budgetbooks

PIANO / VOCAL / GUITAR

BLUES SONGS

ISBN 978-1-4234-3619-5

7777 W. BLUEMOUND RD. P.O. BOX 13819 MILWAUKEE, WI 53213

Visit Hal Leonard Online at
www.halleonard.com

CONTENTS

4 All Your Love (I Miss Loving)

10 As the Years Go Passing By

7 Baby Please Don't Go

14 Beautician Blues

20 Before You Accuse Me (Take a Look at Yourself)

24 Big Boss Man

17 Blues Before Sunrise

26 The Blues Is Alright

32 Blues with a Feeling

38 Bo Diddley

35 Boogie Chillen No. 2

42 Boom Boom

44 Boom Boom (Out Go the Lights)

50 Born Under a Bad Sign

54 Bright Lights, Big City

56 Bring It On Home

66 Built for Comfort

68 Caldonia (What Makes Your Big Head So Hard?)

74 Catfish Blues

61 Cold Shot

76 Come On in My Kitchen

81 Crosscut Saw

84 Cryin' Won't Help You

88 Damn Right, I've Got the Blues

91 Darlin' You Know I Love You

94 Don't Throw Your Love on Me So Strong

97 Double Trouble

100 Dust My Broom

106 Early in the Mornin'

103 Easy Baby

108 Everyday I Have the Blues

114 Five Long Years

116 Further On up the Road

124 Give Me Back My Wig

128 Good Morning Little Schoolgirl

132 Got My Mo Jo Working

134 Got to Hurry

138 Have You Ever Loved a Woman

140 Help the Poor

144 Honest I Do

150 Honey Bee

147 I Ain't Got You

154 I Ain't Superstitious

156 I Can't Quit You Baby

158 I Just Want to Make Love to You

160 I'm a Man

164 I'm Tore Down

170 I'm Your Hoochie Coochie Man

173 Ice Cream Man

178 If You Love Me Like You Say

182 It Hurts Me Too

190 It Serves Me Right to Suffer

192 It's My Own Fault Darlin'

185 Kansas City

194 Key to the Highway

196 Kidney Stew Blues

200 Killing Floor

203 Kind Hearted Woman Blues

206 Let Me Love You Baby

210 Let the Good Times Roll

218 Little Red Rooster

213 Lonesome Whistle Blues

220 Love in Vain Blues

230 Mary Had a Little Lamb

225 Matchbox

234 Messin' with the Kid

236 Move It On Over

238 My Babe

244 My First Wife Left Me

241 Nobody Knows You When You're Down and Out

246 Oh! Darling

250 Paying the Cost to Be the Boss

254 Please Accept My Love

258 Pride and Joy

268 Ramblin' on My Mind

274 Reconsider Baby

278 Rock Me Baby

280 Route 66

265 See See Rider

284 The Sky Is Crying

288 Smokestack Lightning

291 Smoking Gun

294 Someday, After Awhile (You'll Be Sorry)

297 Statesboro Blues

302 (They Call It) Stormy Monday (Stormy Monday Blues)

304 Stormy Weather (Keeps Rainin' All the Time)

308 Sweet Home Chicago

315 Sweet Sixteen

320 Texas Flood

322 The Things That I Used to Do

328 Third Degree

325 Three Hours Past Midnight

330 The Thrill Is Gone

336 Trouble in Mind

340 Tupelo (Tupelo Blues)

333 Wang Dang Doodle

350 Why I Sing the Blues

342 You Shook Me

346 You Upset Me Baby

ALL YOUR LOVE
(I Miss Loving)

Words and Music by
OTIS RUSH

Fm
All your kiss I miss kiss - ing.
I have in store for you.
C7
Be - fore I met you, ba - by,
Well, I love you, ba - by,
B♭m
Fm
I did - n't know what I was miss - ing.
I know you love me too.
1
2
3
To next strain
Fine
All my love, pret - ty
Oh, Oh, Oh,

Swing tempo
F
ba - by,
You know I love you.
Yeah, yeah, yeah,
ba - by,
Bb7
you know I love you,
F
ba - by.
C7
I love you, ba - by,
Bb7
oh, I love you so.
F
Slower
N.C.
D.S. al Fine
(Verse 1)
All your love I miss

BABY PLEASE DON'T GO

Words and Music by
JOSEPH LEE WILLIAMS

G
D7
love you so.
please don't go.
Be - fore I
You know your
G
be your dog,
man done gone,
be - fore I
you know your
be your dog,
man done gone,
be - fore I
you know your
C7
B♭7
be your dog, I get you 'way out here, I may be
man done gone down the coun - ty line, be - fore the

G D7

1

wrong no more. Turn the

sher - iff come.

2 D7 G

You phoned me 'way down here,

you phoned me 'way down here, you phoned me

C7 B♭7 G

'way down here a - bout a roll - ing stone, but you could come down here.

AS THE YEARS GO PASSING BY

Words and Music by
DEADRIC MALONE

Cm
cry.
There is
Fm
noth - in' I can do,
as you leave me here to
Cm
cry.
You know my
G7
love will fol - low you
A♭7
G7
as the years go pass - in'

Cm
by.
2. Give you
...end solo) 4. Gon - na
Verses 2, 4, 6, & 7:
Fm
all that I own;
(4.7.) leave it up to you.
6. (Inst. solo ad lib....
that's one thing you can't de -
So long, so long, good -
Cm
ny.
bye.
Give you
Gon - na
Fm
all that I own;
leave it up to you.
that's one thing you can't de -
So long, so long, good -

Cm
ny.
bye.
You know my
G7
To Coda
A♭7
G7
love will fol - low you
as the years go pass - in'
Cm
1.2.
3.
D.S. al Coda
by.
...end solo) 7. Gon - na
Coda
A♭7
Rubato
G7
Cm
B♭/C
Cm
as the years go pass - in' by.
molto rit.
a tempo
rit.

BEAUTICIAN BLUES

Words and Music by B.B. KING
and JULES BIHARI

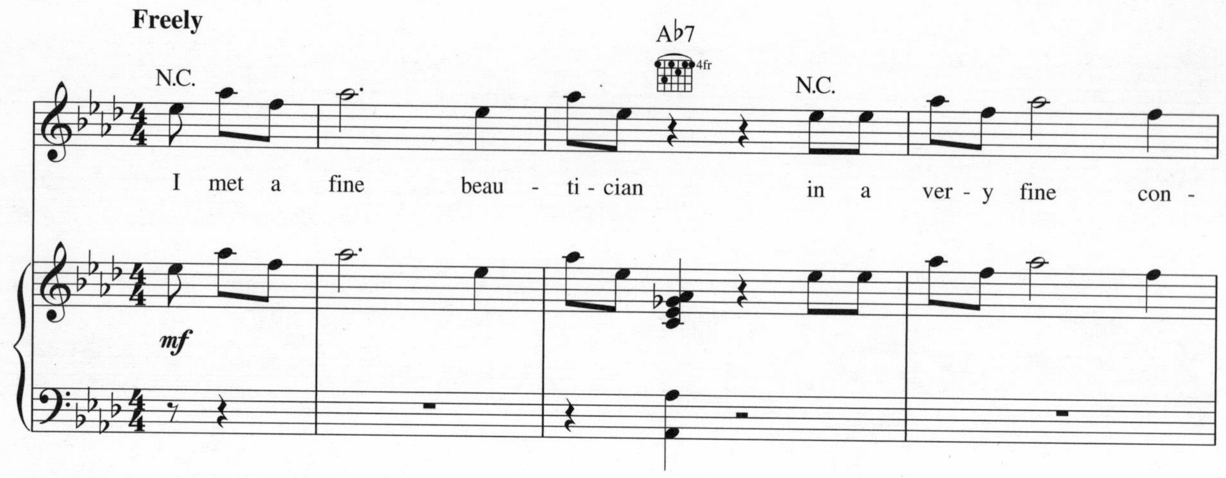

E♭7
She makes a lot of mon - ey, I
D♭7
A♭7
E♭7
don't have to wor - ry 'bout a thing.
She works
A♭7
hard all day, dress - in' hair. Man,
fin - est wom - en from ev - 'ry - where be -
Instrumental solo
keeps her hair so neat and fine, and
you can bet I wan - na get some - where with my
cause my ba - by dress their hair. I'll
ev - 'ry pound of her is mine. I'll

D♭7
4fr
A♭7
4fr
good lov - in' ma - ma, my hard work - in' wom - an.
be a lov - er boy. She treats me like a king.
be her lov - er boy. I'll be hap - py as a king.
E♭7
She makes a lot of mon - ey, I
D♭7
4fr
1-3
A♭7
4fr
E♭7
don't have to wor - ry 'bout a thing.
I meet the
Instrumental solo
Well, she
4
A♭7
4fr
thing.

BLUES BEFORE SUNRISE

Words and Music by
LEROY CARR

owned.
Such a
My
For
F7
E♭7
hard up feel - in',
wife done left me
sev - en long years
boy, I sure de - spise.
for an - oth - er man.
I tried to get a -
B♭
Play 3 times
long.
Sev-en long years,
Lord knows I tried.

Ev - 'ry-thing I could
to get a - long with my
wife, oh; blues be-fore sun - rise
tears stand-in' in my eyes.
F7
Such a hard up feel - in',
E♭7
B♭
boy, I sure de - spise.

BEFORE YOU ACCUSE ME
(Take a Look at Yourself)

Words and Music by
ELLAS McDANIELS

E7
self.
go.
You said "I'm
Your
B7
A7
spend-in' my mon-ey on oth-er wom-en. Your tak-in' mon-ey from some-one else."
ma-ma said, "Son, don't call my daugh-ter no more."
E7
1
B7
2
B7
I
Be-
E7
A7
1.,3. fore you ac-cuse me, take a look at your
2. Come on back home, ba-by. Try my love one more

E7
A7
self.
time.
Be - fore you ac - cuse me,
Come on back home, ba-by.
E7
take a look at your - self.
Try my love one more time.
You say I'm
You know I don't
B7
A7
spend-in' my mon-ey on oth-er wom-en.
know when to quit you.
Your tak - in' mon - ey from some-one else.
I'm gon - na lose my mind.
E7
B7
Ro-bert!
Instrumental solo

A7
E7
A7
E7
B7
A7
To Coda
E7
1
B7
2
B7
D.S. al Coda
Solo ends
Solo ends
Be -
CODA
E7
no chord
E9

BIG BOSS MAN

Words and Music by AL SMITH
and LUTHER DIXON

Eb7 Eb6 Bb Eb9 Bb7 Bb6 Ab Ab7 Ab6
You know you ain't so big, You're just tall that's
Eb Eb6 Eb7 Eb6 Bb7 Ahead to Verse Eb Fine
all.
Well you
Well I'm
Well you
Verse:
Eb Eb6 Eb7 Eb6 Eb Eb6 Eb7 Eb6 Eb
got me work-ing, ba - by, work - ing 'round the clock. I
gon - ng get a Boss Man, one that treats me right.
got me high ba - by, got me wor - ried too,
Eb Eb6 Eb7 Eb6 Eb7 Eb6 A9
want a lit - tle drink of wa - ter but you won't let Jim-my stop. Big Boss
work hard in the day rest - ing at night. Big Boss
Tell me, tell me, tell me what you're gon-na do? Big Boss

THE BLUES IS ALRIGHT

Words and Music by
MILTON CAMPBELL

B♭7
E♭7
I've got this song I'm gon - na
have some -
left me, she gave me the
sing. I'm gon - na sing it just for
one that meant the whole world to me.
blues. That was the last thing I thought I could
A♭7
4fr
you. If you need the blues,
But she left me for some - one else,
use. But now I'm glad she left me.
E♭7
I want you to help me sing it, too.
left my heart in mis - er - y.
I'm glad she gave me the blues.
3

B♭7
I want ev - 'ry - bod - y to hear me when I say
That's when I found out the blues
You see I went out and found me,
A♭7
1, 2
E♭7
that the blues is back and it's here to stay.
would al - ways be a part of me.
I went and found me some - one
B♭7
3
E♭7
B♭7
I used to new.
When she
E♭7
Hey, hey, the blues is al-right. Hey, hey, the
Instrumental solo ad lib.

A♭7
4fr
blues is al - right. Hey, hey, the blues is al - right.
E♭7
B♭7
Hey, hey, the blues is al - right. It's al - right, it's al -
A♭7
4fr
To Coda
1, 2
E♭7
B♭7
right ev-'ry day and night.
3
E♭7
B♭7
night.
I'm

E♭7
glad she left me. I'm
glad she gave me the blues. You see, I'm
A♭7
4fr
grate - ful to the blues. It was the blues that brought me to
E♭7
you. You see, if she had

B♭7
A♭7
4fr
nev - er giv - en me the blues,
I nev - er would have found some - one
E♭7
B♭7
D.S. al Coda
sweet like you.
CODA
E♭7
B♭7
night.
It's al - right, it's al -
A♭7
4fr
E♭7
B♭7 E♭7♯9
right ev-'ry day and night.

BLUES WITH A FEELING

Words and Music by
WALTER JACOBS

A
D7
A
Blues with a feel-ing, that's what I have to-day.
Instrumental solo
What a lone-some feel-ing when you're by your-self.
D7
Blues with a feel-ing, that's what I have to-day.
What a lone-some feel-ing when you're by your-self.
A
E7
I'm gon-na find my ba-by
When the one that you're lov-in'
D7
A
1, 2
A
E7
if it takes all night and day.
has gone a-way and left.
Solo ends

3
A
E7
A7
Well, you know I love you, ba - by. I won-der the rea - son why, you
told me you loved me, ba - by, and you left me here to cry.
D7
Blues with a feel - ing,
A
that's what I have to - day,
I'm gon - na
E7
D7
A
A7
find my ba - by, if it takes all night and day.

BOOGIE CHILLEN NO. 2

Words and Music by JOHN LEE HOOKER
and BERNARD BESMAN

A♭7
back.
I'm a
E♭7
man now, ba - by, and I sure can have my fun.
A♭7
My ba - by got some-thin'
round like an ap - ple, shaped like a pear. Sure

D♭7
now, babe. My ba - by got some-thin'. My ba -
A♭
- by got some - thin'. My ba -
E♭7
- by got some - thin', man, I sure do love.
A♭
A7
A♭

BO DIDDLEY

Words and Music by
ELLAS McDANIEL

G
G6
G
If that pri - vate eye can't see,
he bet - ter not take that
3
3
Dm7
G
ring from me.
Bo Did - dl - ey caught a nan - ny goat, _
3
3
to make his pret - ty ba - by a Sun - day coat. _
R.H.
Bo Did - dl - ey caught a bear - cat,
3
3
R.H.

To make his pret - ty ba - by a Sun - day hat.
R.H.
Dm7
G
ff
Dm7
G
Dm7
G
N.C.
G6
mf
G
G6
Won't you come to my house and rack that bone,
mp

G
G6
G
take my ba-by all the way from home.
Look at that bo-do, oh,
G6
G
where's he been,
up to your house and gone a-gain.
G6
G
Bo Did-dl-ey, Bo Did-dl-ey, have you heard,
R.H.
Repeat and Fade
my pret-ty ba-by said she was a bird.
R.H.

BOOM BOOM

Words and Music by
JOHN LEE HOOKER

G7
F7
C
1.2.
Love that is true,
Boom, boom, boom, boom.
2. I like the way you
You knock me out,
Right off my feet.
3. I need you right
Come on, come on,
Come shake it up, baby.
3.
C
C6
(Group:)
(Shake it, baby)
(Shake it,
Come on and shake,
Shake it up, baby,
mf (Repeat and fade at end)
F7
C
baby)
(Shake it, baby)
(Shake it,
Come on, now, baby,
I don't mean maybe,
G7
F7
baby)
(Shake it, baby)
You're drivin' me crazy,
Come on, come on.
Come on, come on,
All right, all right.
1. C
2. C
(Shake it, baby)
(Shake it, baby)
Come on and

BOOM BOOM
(Out Go the Lights)

Words and Music by
STANLEY LEWIS

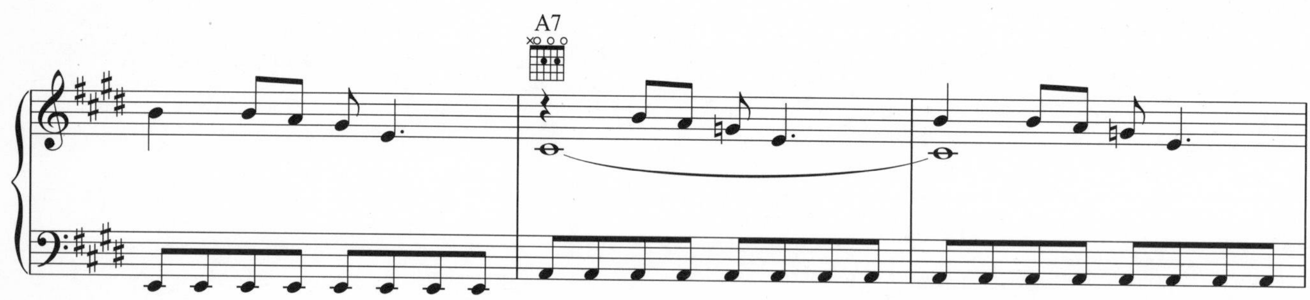

B13
7fr

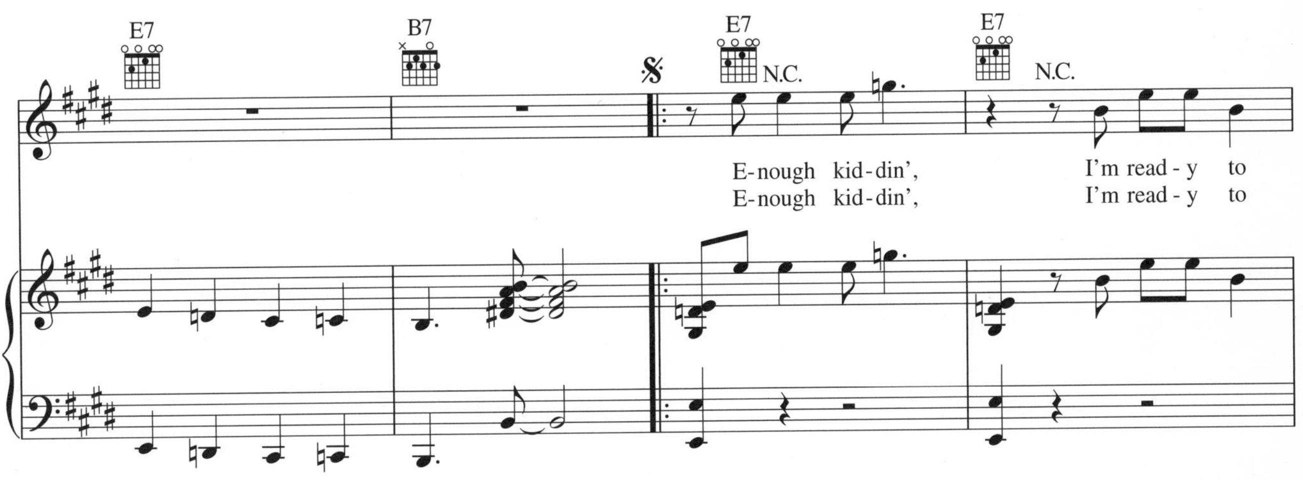
E7
B7
E7
N.C.
E7
N.C.
E-nough kid-din', I'm read-y to
E-nough kid-din', I'm read-y to

E7
N.C.
fight. I've been look-in' for my ba-by all night.
go. If I find her, boy, don't you know.

A7
E7
N.C.
If I get her in my sight, boom boom, out go the lights.
B13
7fr
E7
To Coda
1
B7
2
B7
E7
Well, I thought I treat - ed my ba - by fair, but I
just found out she don't want me here.
A7
If I get her in

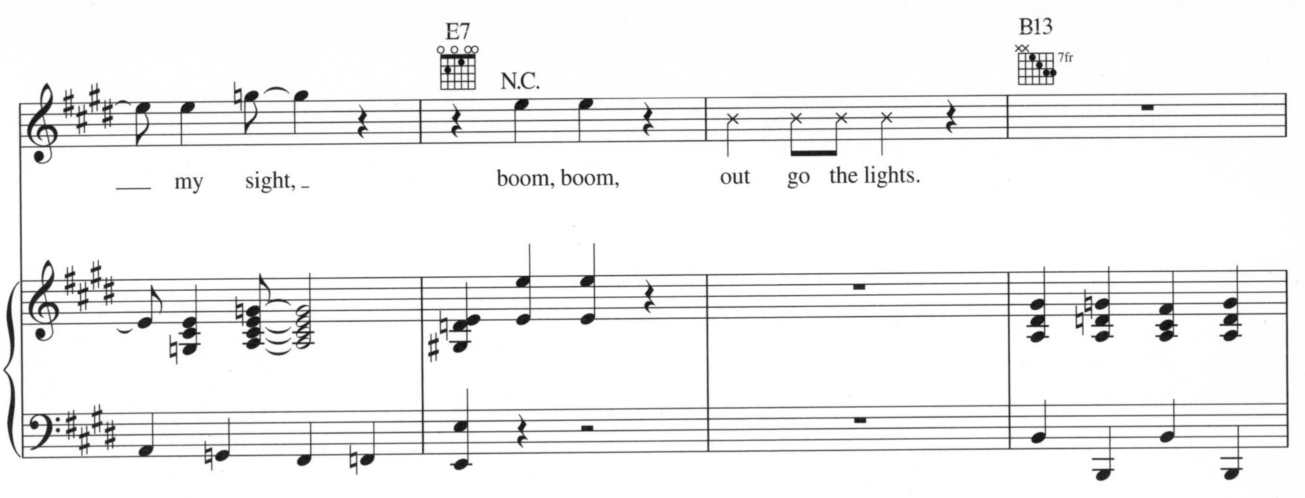
E7
N.C.
B13
7fr
my sight,
boom, boom,
out go the lights.

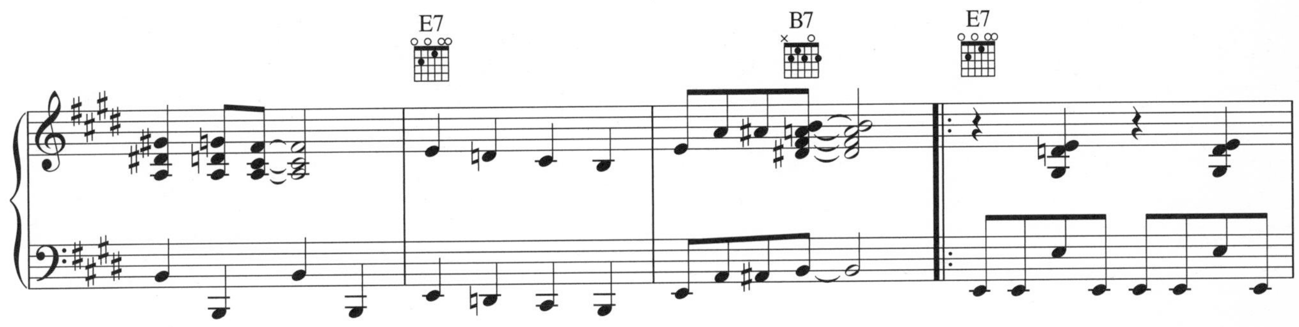
E7
B7
E7

A7

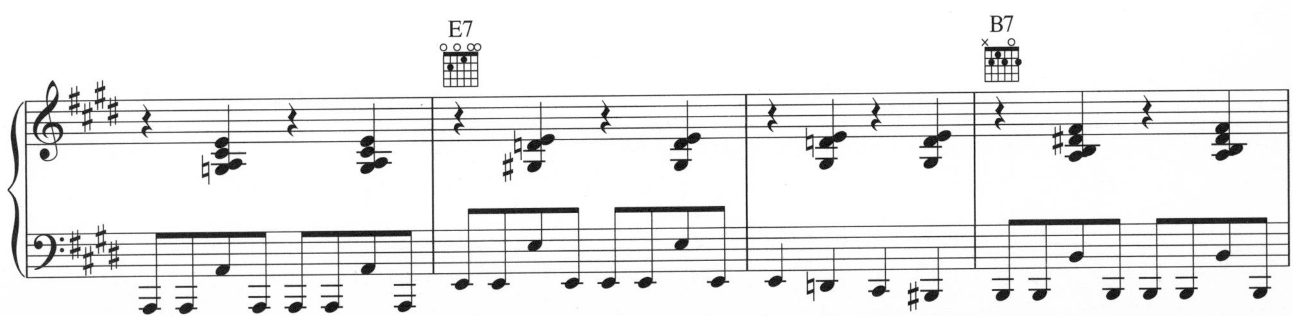
E7
B7

A7
E7
1
B7
2
B7
E7
Well, I never felt this mad before. But I
just found out she don't want me no more.
A7
If I get her in
my sight,
E7
N.C.
boom boom, out go the lights!

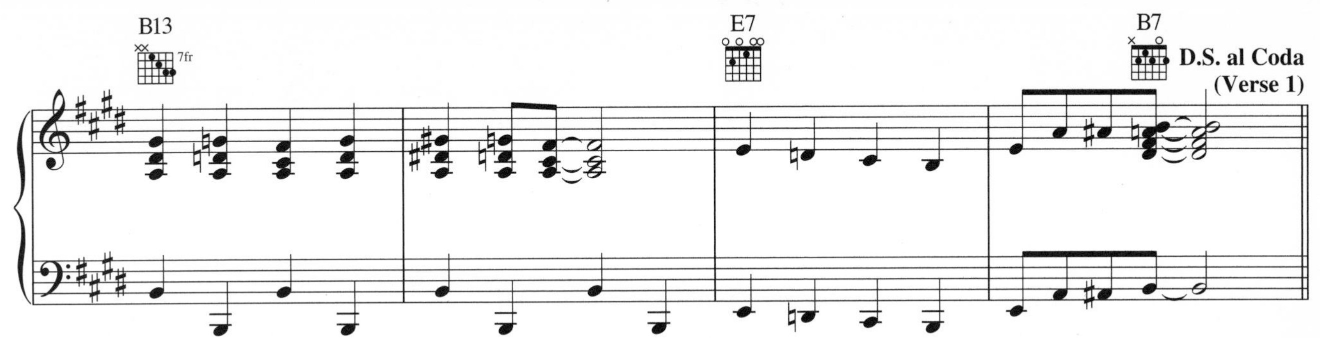
B13
7fr
E7
B7
D.S. al Coda
(Verse 1)

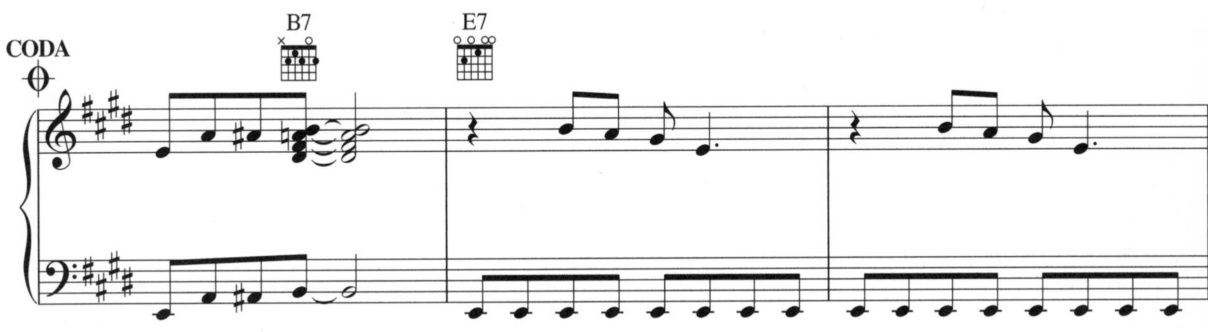
CODA
B7
E7

A7

N.C.
E7

BORN UNDER A BAD SIGN

Words and Music by BOOKER T. JONES
and WILLIAM BELL

Am
Born un-der a bad sign;
been down since I be-gan to crawl.
E
D
Am
Bm
Oh, if it was-n't for bad luck,
I would-n't have no luck at all.
(Let me tell you.)
Am
Bm
Am
Hard luck and trou - ble
I can't read; I nev - er
Wine and wom - en is
is my on - ly friend;
been on my own ev - er since I was ten.
learned how to write.
My whole life has been one big fight.
all I crave;
a big-head wom-an will car ry me to my grave.

Am
Born un-der a bad sign; been down _ since I be - gan to crawl.
E
D
Am
Oh, if it was - n't for bad ___ luck, _ I would-n't have no luck at all.
Bm
Am
To Coda
Bm
Am
Bm
I've often heard the old folks say,
Am
Bm
Am
"Don't give up, when the chips are down, you got to keep on pushing." So I

Bm
Am
Bm
guess I gotta keep on pushing. You see, I was down, but I
Am
Bm
Am
kind of picked myself up a little bit, oh, and I had to dust myself off,
Bm
Am
Bm
Am
clean myself up, and now, I'm gonna keep on pushing; I can't stop.
N.C.
D.S. al Coda
CODA
Am
Bm
Repeat and Fade
Optional Ending
Am7
(Spoken ad lib.)
I'm gonna get myself together now,
I'm gonna keep on pushing.

BRIGHT LIGHTS, BIG CITY

Words and Music by
JIMMY REED

G Dm7 G Dm7 G Dm7
right, Pret-ty ba-by, Gon-na need my help some-
G Dm7 C B♭ C B♭
day, All right, Pret-ty ba-by, Gon-na
G Dm7 G6 Dm7 D Cmaj7
need my help some-day. You gon-na wish you had list-en'd to
B♭maj7 G6 Dm7 G6 Dm7
some of the things that I say. Bright
G6 Dm7 G6 Dm7 G6 Dm7 G6 Dm7
say.
Repeat and fade out.

BRING IT ON HOME

Written by
WILLIE DIXON

3
I'm gon - na
bring it on home to you.
I done
I
bought my tick - et, I got my load.
think a - bout the good times I once have had.
Con - duc -

- tor hol - lered, "All a - board."
Soul got hap - py, heart got glad.
A7
Take my seat, ride way back,
I think a - bout the way you love me, too.
and
You can

E7
watch this train move down the track.
bet your life I'm com - in' home to you.
1
2
I'm gon - na bring it on home.
I'm gon - na bring it on home, now.

A7
I'm gon - na bring it on home, now.
E7
Gon - na bring it on home, now.
B7
Gon - na bring it on home,
A7
E7
bring it on home to you.

COLD SHOT

Words and Music by MIKE KINDRED
and WESLEY CLARK

But now I reach to kiss your lips, my
But now I see you out some - where, you
N.C.
touch don't mean a thing.
won't give me the time of day.
D
And that's a cold shot, ba - by.
Am
Yeah, that's a drag.
A cold shot,
D
ba - by.
E7♯9
6fr
I let our love go
We let our love go

1, 2
Am
bad.
bad.
3
Am
End instrumental
I real-ly meant I was sor-ry for ev-er caus-in' you pain.
You showed your ap-pre-ci-a-tion

D
by walk - in' out an - y - way.
And that's a cold shot,
ba - by.
Am
Yeah, that's a drag.
And that's a cold shot,
D
ba - by.
E7♯9
6fr
We let our love go
Am
bad.

E7♯9
6fr
Am
A7♯9
6fr

BUILT FOR COMFORT

Written by
WILLIE DIXON

A7
E7
To Coda
But I got ev-'ry - thing,
D7
A7
all that a good girl need.
1
E7
2
E7
3
E7
D.S. al Coda
Some folk
Solo ends
I ain't
CODA
D7
A7
B♭7 A7
all you good wom-en need.

CALDONIA
(What Makes Your Big Head So Hard?)

Words and Music by
FLEECIE MOORE

F7
C
G7
C
G

G
Walk-in' with mah ba - by, she's got great big feet. She's long, lean and lank - y, ain't had
noth - in' to eat. But she's my
C7
ba - by and I love her just the
G
same.
D7
Cra - zy 'bout that wom - an 'cause Cal -
don - ia is her
G
name. Cal -

N.C.
do - nia! Cal - do - nia! What makes your big head so
C
hard? But I love you, love you just the
G
D7
same. Cra - zy 'bout that wom - an 'cause Cal -
G
do - nia is her name.

(Spoken:) My mama told me to leave Caldonia alone: "She's bad for your morale."
C9
But mama didn't know I loved Caldonia. She's
G
such a swell gal!
D9(add11)
5fr
So, I'm goin' down to
D7
G
Caldonia's house and ask her just one more time.
Cal -

N.C.
do - nia! Cal - do - nia! What makes your big head so hard?
C9
G
Am7
D7
G

CATFISH BLUES

Words and Music by
ROBERT PETWAY

Additional Lyrics

6. Well, now I know, I know you don't want me.
Why in the world won't you tell me so?
Then I won't be caught, baby, 'round
Your house no more,
Your house no more,
Your house no more.

COME ON IN MY KITCHEN

Words and Music by
ROBERT JOHNSON

B♭
Ah, the wom-an I love, took from my best
friend. Some jok-er got luck-y, stole he back a-gain. You bet-ter come
on in my kitch-en, babe, it's gon' to be rain-in' out-doors.
Aw, she's

B♭
gone, I know she won't come back. ___ I've taken the last nick - el ___ out of her _ na - tion
sack. You bet-ter come on in my kitch - en, babe, it's
gon' to be rain - in' out - doors. ___ (Spoken:) Baby, can't you hear that wind howl?
Oh, can't you hear that wind howl? You bet-ter come

on in my kitch - en, ba - by, it's gon' to be rain - in' out - doors.
When a wom - an gets in
B♭
trou - ble, ev-'ry bod - y throws her down. Look - in' for her good friend, none can be
found. You bet - ter come on in my kitch - en, ba - by, it's

gon' to be rain - in' out - doors.
B♭
Win-ter time's com - in', it's gon' be slow. You can't make the
win-ter, babe, that's dry long so. You bet-ter come on in my kitch-
en, 'cause it's gon' to be rain - in' out-doors.

CROSSCUT SAW

Words and Music by
R.G. FORD

A
cross cut saw, baby, drag me a-cross your log.
D
I'm a cross cut saw, baby, drag me a-cross
A
E7
your log. I'll cut your wood so eas-y for you
D
A
you can't help but say, "Hot Dog!" Some

A
call me Wood-cut-ting Sam, some call me Wood-cut-ting Jim, the last girl I cut wood for, she wants
dou-ble blade axe that real-ly cuts good. I'm a cross cut saw that will bur-
me back a-gain. Well, I'm a cross cut saw, ba-by, drag me a-cross
-y in your wood. I'm a cross cut saw, ba-by, drag me a-cross
D
3
your log. I'll cut your wood so eas-y for you,
your log. I'll cut your wood so eas-y for you,
E7
you can't help but say, "Hot Dog!" I've got a
you can't help but say, "Hot Dog!"
1.
2.
D.C. and fade

CRYIN' WON'T HELP YOU

Words and Music by B.B. KING
and SAUL BIHARI

mat - ter what you say, babe, no mat - ter what you do, the
must re - mem - ber, ba - by, no mat - ter where you go,
way you treat me, wom - an, I just can't un - der - stand. I'm
just be - fore I leave you, just wan - na shake your hand. I'm
way you've been treat - in' me, wom - an, is com - in' back home to you.
watch those seeds you scat - ter, wom - an, 'cause you're gon - na reap what you sow.
gon - na leave you, wom - an and let you do the best you can.
gon - na get me a wom - an, babe, not to get you mad.
And your
F7
cry - in' won't help you, wom - an. Oh, cry - in' won't help you,
C7
babe. Oh,

G7
F7
To Coda
3
cry - in' won't help you, wom - an, 'cause you've been so mean to
C7
1, 2
me.
Oh, you
Oh, the
3

F7
C7
G7
F7
C7
D.S. al Coda
Oh,
CODA
C7
N.C.
me.
D♭9
C7

DAMN RIGHT, I'VE GOT THE BLUES

By BUDDY GUY

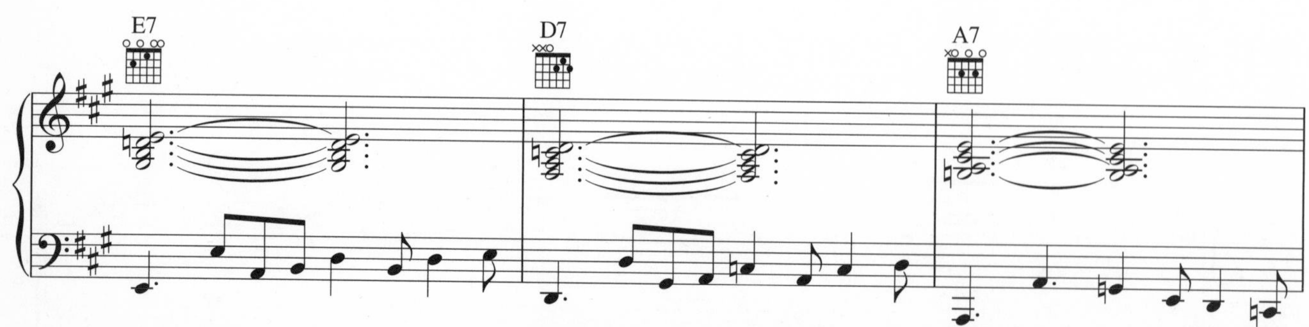

(1., 4.) You're damn right I got the blues
stopped by my daugh-ter's house,
Instrumental solo
from my head down to my shoes.
you know I just want to use the phone.
D7
You're damn right I got the blues
I stopped by my daugh-ter's house,
A7
from my head down to my shoes.
you know I just want to use the phone.

E7
I can't win
You know my new grand-ba-by came to the door,
D7
A7
'cause I don't have a thing to lose.
and said, "Grand-dad-dy, you know ain't no one at home."
1-3
4
(2.) I
(4.) You're
You're damn right I've got the
blues.
You're damn right I've got the blues.

DARLIN' YOU KNOW I LOVE YOU

Words and Music byB.B. KING
and JULES BIHARI

To Coda
B♭m7
E♭7
A♭
B♭m7
D♭
D7
E♭7
left me for some-one else.
I
A♭
A♭7
D♭
think of you, think of you ev-'ry morn-ing, and dream of you ev-'ry
Instrumental solo to end
D♭m
G♭7
A♭
F7
B♭m7
E♭7
A♭
B♭m7
night. And would love, love to be with you al-ways.
A♭7
D♭
D♭m
When night be-gins to fall, I

A♭
A♭7
B♭7
cry, cry a - lone. And I wish, ba - by, I could
B♭m7
1
E♭7
hold you in my arms to - night. Oh,
2
E♭7
D.S. al Coda
CODA
A♭
G♭
F7
N.C.
B♭m7/E♭
A♭
D♭
A♭
A♭7

DON'T THROW YOUR LOVE ON ME SO STRONG

Words and Music by
ALBERT KING

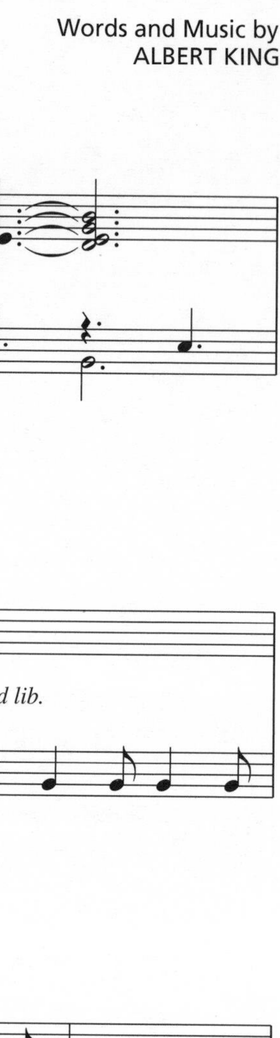

Bb7
F7
Eb7
Bb7
Eb7
Bb7
F+
Bb7
Hey ba - by,
Hey ba - by,
Hey ba - by,
Eb7
Bb7
F+
don't throw your love on me, on me so strong.
I know what you've been put-tin' down.
I like what you've got on your mind.
Bb7
Eb7
Hey ba - by,
Hey ba - by,
Hey ba - by,

B♭7
F+
don't throw your love on me so strong.
I know what you've been put - tin' down.
I like what you've got on your mind.
B♭7
F7
They tell me your love's like a fau - cet,
You came by and saw me last Tues - day,
And ev - 'ry time you love me,
E♭7
B♭7
E♭7
you can turn it off and on.
Lord, you said you did-n't want, want me a -
Well, our love al-most drives me stone blind.
1,2
B♭7
F7
3
B♭7
F+
B♭7
round.

DOUBLE TROUBLE

Words and Music by
OTIS RUSH

A7
Gm7
gen-er-a-tion of mill-ion-aires, it's hard for me to keep de-cent clothes to wear.
Dm
You laughed at me walk-in,'
ba-by when I had no place to go.
Bad luck and trou-ble have tak-en me
I have got no mon-ey to show.
Hey,

Gm
Dm
hey, to make it you've got to try,
ba - by
that's no lie.
A7
Yes in this gen-er - a - tion of mill - ion-aires,
it's
Gm7
Dm
hard for me to keep de-cent clothes to wear.
Gm
A7
Dm
rit.

DUST MY BROOM

Words and Music by ELMORE JAMES
and ROBERT JOHNSON

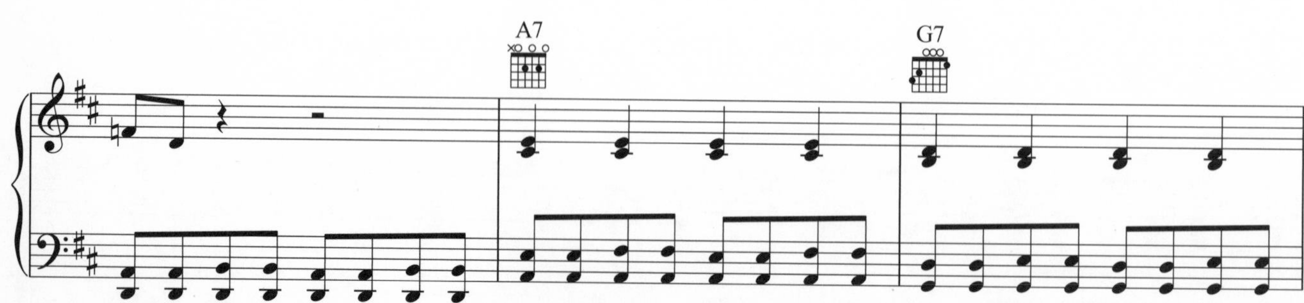

D7
A7
I'm get - tin' up
D7
G7
soon in the morn - in'. I be - lieve I'll dust my
write a let - ter, tel - e - phone ev - 'ry town I
want no wom - an want ev - 'ry down - town man she
lieve, I be - lieve my time ain't
Instrumental solo
broom. I'm get - tin' up
know. I'm gon - na
meets. No, I don't
long. I be -
G7
soon in the morn - in'. I be - lieve I'll dust my
write a let - ter, tel - e - phone ev - 'ry town I
want no wom - an want ev - 'ry down - town man she
lieve, I be - lieve my time ain't

D7
broom. Out with the
know. If I don't
meets. Man, she's a
long. I ain't gon - na
A7
G7
best gal, I'm lov - in' her. Now my friends can get to my
find her in Mis - sis - sip - pi, she's in West Mem - phis I
no good wom - an, 'less she's back out on the
leave my ba - by and break up my hap - py
1-4
D7
A7
room.
know.
street.
home.
(2.) I'm gon - na
(3.) And I don't
(4.) I be -
(5.)
5
D7
D♭/E♭
D

EASY BABY

Written by
WILLIE DIXON

C7
day.
You don't have to
You don't have to
work all day. Just make love to me and say
weep and moan. Just hold me, baby, in your arms.
F7
C7
eas - y, ba - by, eas - y, ba - by.
(2.,3.) Eas - y, ba - by, eas - y, ba - by.
G7
F7
Eas - y, ba - by, oh, you love me night and
Eas - y, ba - by, let me love you night and

C7
To Coda
1
day.
day.
2
D.S. al Coda
CODA
Repeat and Fade

EARLY IN THE MORNIN'

Words and Music by LEO HICKMAN,
LOUIS JORDAN and DALLAS BARTLEY

I went to all the pla-ces where we used to go Went
I went to see her girl friend but she was out I
had a lot of mon - ey when I start - ed out I
Eb7
Ab7
to her house but she did-n't live there no more
knock'd on her moth-er's door and how she did shout
could-n't find my ba-by, now my mon-ey's run out
Now it's EAR - LY IN THE MORN - IN'
Eb7
Bb7
It's EAR - LY IN THE MORN-IN'
It's EAR - LY IN THE MORN-IN' and I
Ab7
Eb
1,2
D. S. al Fine
3
Fine
ain't got noth-in' but the blues
I
I

EVERYDAY I HAVE THE BLUES

Words and Music by
PETER CHATMAN

G
ev - 'ry - day I have the blues;
well, you
A7
D7
see me wor - ry, ba - by,
be - cause it's you I hate to
G
lose.
No - bod - y loves me,
C7
G
G7
no - bod - y seems to care,
no - bod - y

C7
G
loves me, no-bod-y seems to care;
A7
D7
Speak-in' of bad luck and trou-ble, well, you know I've had my
G
share.
I'm gon-na pack my suit-case,
C7
G
G7
mov-in' on down the line,
oh,

C7
G
I'm gon - na pack my suit - case, move on down the
A7
D7
line; well there ain't no - bod - y wor - ryin' and there ain't no - bod - y
G
cryin'. Seems to me ev - 'ry - day, ev - 'ry -
G7
day, ev - 'ry - day I have the blues, ev - 'ry -

C7
G
day, ev - 'ry - day, ev - 'ry - day, ev - 'ry - day I have the blues.
Am7
D7
Bbdim7
D7
You see me wor - ry, ba - by, 'cause it's you I hate to lose.
Fine
G
Gdim7
Am7
Abmaj7
G
No -
- bod - y loves me, no -

G7
- bod - y seems to care; no -
C7
- - bod - y loves me, no -
G
- bod - y seems to care; speak - in' of bad luck and trou - ble,
A7
D7
G
D.S. al Fine
well, you know I've my share. Ev - 'ry -

FIVE LONG YEARS

Words and Music by
EDDIE BOYD

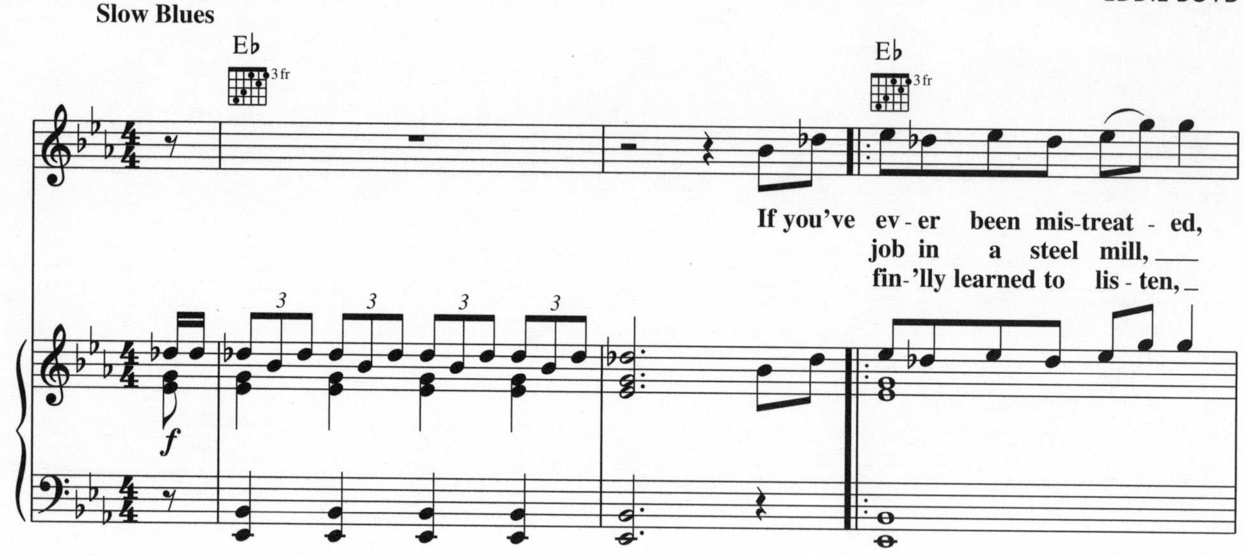

N.C.
bout.
pay.
gold.
I worked five long years for one wom - an,
and she had the nerve to put me out.
1, 2
Got a
I
3
E♭
3 fr

FURTHER ON UP THE ROAD

Words and Music by JOE VEASEY
and DON ROBEY

C9

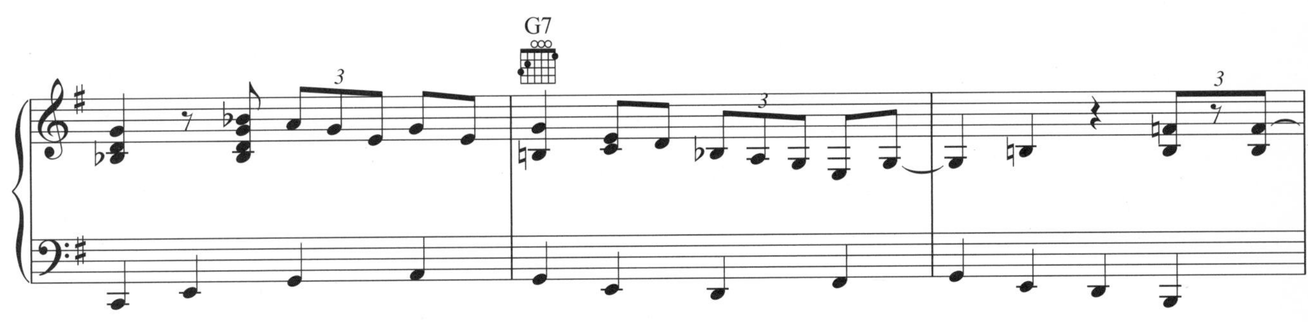
G7

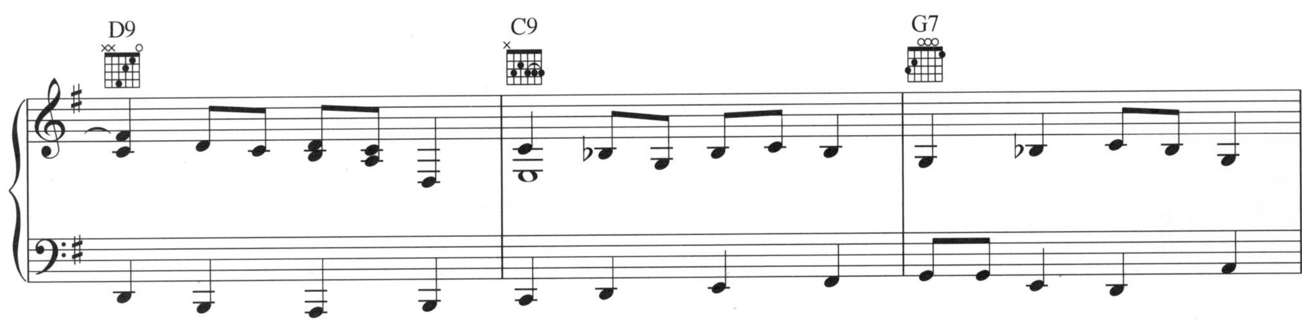
D9
C9
G7

Fur-ther on up the road
some - bod-y's gon-na hurt you

C9
like you hurt me.
Fur - ther on up the road
G7
some - bod - y's gon - na hurt you like you hurt me.
Fur - ther on
D9
C9
G7
up the road,
ba - by, just you wait and see.
Now you're laugh - in', pret - ty ba - by,
pret - ty soon you're gon - na be

C9
cry - in'.
Now you're laugh - in', pret - ty ba - by,
G7
pret - ty soon you're gon-na be cry - in'.
Fur-ther on
D9
C9
G7
up the road,
you'll find out I was-n't ly - in'.
G7
Guitar solo ad lib.

C9
G7
D9
C9
1
G7
2
G7
G7
Fur - ther on up the road
some - bod - y's gon - na hurt you

C9
like you hurt me.
Fur-ther on up the road
G7
some - bod-y's gon-na hurt you, too.
Fur-ther on up the
D9
C9
G7
road
some - bod-y's gon-na hurt you, too.
G7
Guitar solo ad lib.

C9
G7
D9
C9
1
G7
2
G7
Fur-ther on up the road.
G7
Fur - ther on up the road.

C9
Fur - ther on up the road.
Fur - ther on up the road.
G7
D9
Fur - ther on up the road
C9
G7
you're gon - na find out I was-n't ly - in'.
G9

GIVE ME BACK MY WIG

Words and Music by
THEODORE "HOUND DOG" TAYLOR

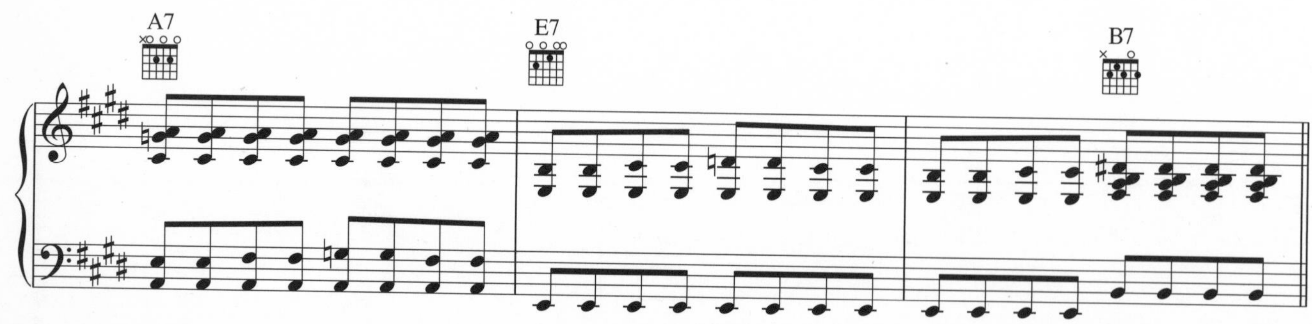

E7
Give me back_ my wig.
Hon-ey, now, let your head go
bald.
A7
Give me back_ my wig.
Hon-ey, now let your head go
E7
bald.

B7
A7
Real - ly did - n't have no bus' - ness
hon - ey, buy - in' you no wig at
E7
B7
all.
E7
Tak - in' Main down - town,
That's what my ma - ma told me,
Instrumental solo
Good - bye, lit - tle wom - an.
Instrumental solo
take off For - ty - ninth.
and your good friend, too.
All I've got to say:
When I get down there, I swear
When you get that wig, that's the way
give me back my wig and be
nine nine - ty nine. You just
you ain't gon - na do. You just
on your mer - ry way. You just

A7
give me back my wig.
Hon-ey, now, let your head go
E7
bald.
B7
Real-ly did-n't have no bus'-ness,
A7
hon-ey, buy-in' you no wig at all.
1-4
E7
B7
5
E7

GOOD MORNING LITTLE SCHOOLGIRL

Words and Music by
SONNY BOY WILLIAMSON

Dm
Can I come home with you?
what in the world to do.
Fly right o - ver the town.

Tell your
Well I
If I

A
G#
G
no chord
moth - er and your pa - pa I once was a
don't want to hurt your feel - ings, or e - ven get
don't find my ba - by ain't gon - na

To Coda
Dm
school - boy too.
mad at you.
put my airplane down.
1,3
2
Some - times I don't
G
Instrumental Solo
Dm

A7
G7
Dm
D.S. al Coda
I'm gon- na buy me an
CODA
Dm

GOT MY MO JO WORKING

Words and Music by
PRESTON FOSTER

C
2. I got my black cat bones all pure and dry, I got a
3. (- Got my) hoo - doo ash - es all a - round your bed, Got my
4. (I got a gyp - sy wom - an giv - ing me ad - vice, I got some
5. (I got my) rab - bit's foot, I know it's work - ing right, I got your
C7
F9
four - leaf clov - er all hang - ing high.
black snake boots un - der - neath your head.
red hot tips I have to keep on ice.
strand of hair, I keep it day and night.
I Got My Mo - Jo Work - ing but it
C
G7
just won't work on you.
Oh, I want to love you so till I
F9
C
1. 2. 3.
4.
C7 add13
don't know what to do.
3. Got my
4. I got a
5. I got my
rall.

GOT TO HURRY

By OSCAR RASPUTIN

A7
E7
D7
A7
D7
A7

E7
D7
A7
E7
A7
D7
A7
E7
D7
A7

1
E7
2
E7
A7
D7
A7
E7
D7
A7
E7
Repeat and Fade
Optional Ending
A7

HAVE YOU EVER LOVED A WOMAN

Words and Music by
BILLY MYLES

2. But you just love that woman so much, it's a shame and a sin.
You just love that woman so much, it's a shame and a sin.
But all the time, you know she belongs to your very best friend.

3. Have you ever loved a woman, oh, you know you can't leave her alone?
Have you ever loved a woman, yes, you know you can't leave her alone?
Something deep inside of you won't let you wreck your best friend's home.

HELP THE POOR

Words and Music by
CHARLIE SINGLETON

Moderate Latin feel ♩ = 100

Dm

mf

𝄋 *Verse:*

Dm

1. Help the poor; won't you help poor

2.3. *See additional lyrics*

A7
need it des - p'rate - ly.
I need you so
Dm
much; I need your care. I need all
Gm
the lov - in', ba - by, you can spare.
To Coda
1.
A7
Dm
Help the poor; oh, ba - by, help poor me.
Dm
2.
A7
2. Say you will; help poor me.

Dm
Bridge:
Gm
You are my in - spi - ra - tion.
Dm
You could make me be a king.
Gm
But, if you don't come to my res - cue,
I could-n't ev - er be an - y - thing.
A7
A7(♯5)
D.S. 𝄋 al Coda
3. Help the poor;

Verse 2:
Say you will; say you'll help me on.
I can't make it no further in this world alone.
Baby, I'm beggin', with tears in my eyes,
For your lovin'; don't you realize?
I need help; oh, baby, help poor me.
(To Bridge:)

Verse 3:
Help the poor; baby, help poor me.
Have a heart, won't you, baby; listen to my plea.
I lost my courage till I found you.
You got what it takes, baby, to pull me through.
Help the poor; oh, baby, won't you help poor me.
(To Coda)

HONEST I DO

Words and Music by JIMMY REED
and EWART G. ABNER, JR.

F
G♯dim7
Gm7
no one a - bove you.
F
N.C.
B♭
Please tell me you love me,
C7
stop driv - ing me mad.
You're the sweet - est lit - tle
wom - an
that I ev - er had.
F
G♯dim7
Gm7

F
N.C.
B♭
Please tell me you love me,
C7
stop driv - ing me mad.
When I woke up this morn - ing,
F
G♯dim7
Gm7
F
nev - er felt so bad.

I AIN'T GOT YOU

Words and Music by
CALVIN CARTER

F7
F
B♭9
Bdim
F7
and no mat - ter where I goes,
you keep the
F
B♭9
Bdim
F7
B♭9
N.C.
ring in my nose,
but I ain't got you.
3
Fdim/G♯
F/A
B♭
B♭dim7
B♭
B♭dim7
B♭
I got a tav - ern
and a li - quor store;
I hit the
B♭dim7
B♭
B♭dim7
B♭
B♭7
E♭9
num - bers,
four for - ty - four.
I got a mo - jo,

C
N.C.
C7
don't you know? I'm all dressed up with no place to go. I got
F
B♭9
Bdim
F7
F
B♭9
Bdim
wom-en to the left of me, I got wom-en to the right of me,
F7
F
B♭9
Bdim
F7
I got wom-en all a-round me, but I
1
B♭9
N.C.
Fdim/G♯
F/A
2
B♭9
N.C.
Fdim/G♯
C7
F
ain't got you. I got a ain't got you.

HONEY BEE

Words and Music by
McKINLEY MORGANFIELD (MUDDY WATERS)

Bb7
Sail on, sail on, my lit-tle hon-ey bee, sail on.
F7
C7
Bb7
(1.) You gon-na keep on sail-in' till you lose your hap-py home.
(2.) I don't mind your sail-in', but please don't sail so long.

1, 2
F7
C7
3
C7
F7
I hear a lot of buzz - ing;
sounds like my lit - tle hon - ey bee.
B♭7
I hear a lot of buzz - ing;

F7
sounds like my lit-tle hon-ey bee.
C7
She been all'round the world mak-in' hon-ey,
B♭7
F7
but now she is com-in' back home to me.
F13
F7

I AIN'T SUPERSTITIOUS

Written by
WILLIE DIXON

F7
C
1
2
I'll prob-a-bly get put in jail.
some-bod y's got to go.
When my
Well, the
F7
C
dogs are all howl-in' all o-ver the neigh-bor - hood.
Well, the
F7
C
dogs are all howl-in' all o-ver the neigh-bor - hood.
That is a
G7
F7
C
true sign of death; ba-by, that ain't no good.

I CAN'T QUIT YOU BABY

Written by
WILLIE DIXON

Additional Lyrics

2. Well, you know I love you, baby; my love for you I can never hide.
   Well, you know I love you, baby; my love for you I can never hide.
   Well, I can't quit you, baby; my love for you I can never hide.

3. When you hear me moanin' and groanin', baby, you know it hurts me deep down inside.
   When you hear me moanin' and groanin', baby, you know it hurts me deep down inside.
   When you hear me moanin', baby, you know you're my one desire.

I JUST WANT TO MAKE LOVE TO YOU

Written by
WILLIE DIXON

1
Eb/Bb
Ab/Bb
Eb
6fr
4fr
3fr
love to you.
2
Eb/Bb
Ab/Bb
Eb
Ab
Bbm7
love to you. I can tell by the way you
Ab/C
Bbm7
Ab
Bbm7
Ab/C
Bbm7
walk that walk, I can hear by the way you talk that talk, I can
Ab
Bbm7
Ab/C
Db
Bb7#5(#9)
know by the way you treat me, girl, that I could give you all the lov - in' in the
D.C. al Coda
whole wide world.
CODA
Eb/Bb
Ab/Bb
Eb
love to you.

I'M A MAN

Words and Music by
ELLAS McDANIEL

G
C
G
C
You know, ba - by, we can have a lot o' fun.
Bring back a sec-ond cous - in, lit - tle John the Con-quer-oo.
3
I'm a man.
I spell M - A -
- N,
Man.
Ah.
Ah.
Ah.
Ah.

G
C
G
C
All you pret - ty wom - en
stand in line.
The line I shoot
will nev - er miss.
I can make love to you, ba - by,
in an ho - ur's time.
The way I make love to 'em,
they came for this
I'm a man.
Spelled M
- A -
- N,
Man.
To Coda

G
C
G
C
G
C
G
C
G
C
G
C
D.S. al Coda
CODA
G
C
G
C
G
C
Ah.
Ah.
Ah.
G
C
G
C
G
Ah.
Oh.

I'M TORE DOWN

Words and Music by
SONNY THOMPSON

G7
F7
Well, I feel like this when my ba - by can't be found.
C7
F
Went to the riv - er
C7
to jump in. My ba - by showed up and said, "I will tell you when." Well, I'm
F7
C7
tore down. al - most lev - el with the ground.

G7
F7
Well, I feel like this when my ba - by can't be found.
C7
C7
I love you, babe, with all my
love you, ba - by, with
C7
D♭7
C7
D♭7
heart and soul. Love like mine will nev - er grow old.
all my might. Love like mine is out of sight. I'll
C7
D♭7
C7
Love you in the morn-ing and in the eve - nin', too. Ev - 'ry time you leave me I get
lie for you if you want me to. I real - ly don't be - lieve that your

F7
mad — with you.
love — is true.
Well, I'm tore down.
I'm al - most lev - el with the
C7
G7
ground.
Well, I feel like this — when my
F7
To Coda
ba - by can't — be found. —
C7
Guitar solo ad lib.

F7

C7
3
G7
3

F7
C7
1
3

2
D.S. al Coda
I

CODA
G7
I'm tore down,
I'm

al - most lev - el with the ground.
Well, I'm
F7
C7
tore down, I'm al - most lev - el with the ground.
G7
Well, I feel like this when my
F7
C
C/E
F
F♯dim
C/G
D♭9
C9
ba - by can't be found.

I'M YOUR HOOCHIE COOCHIE MAN

Written by
WILLIE DIXON

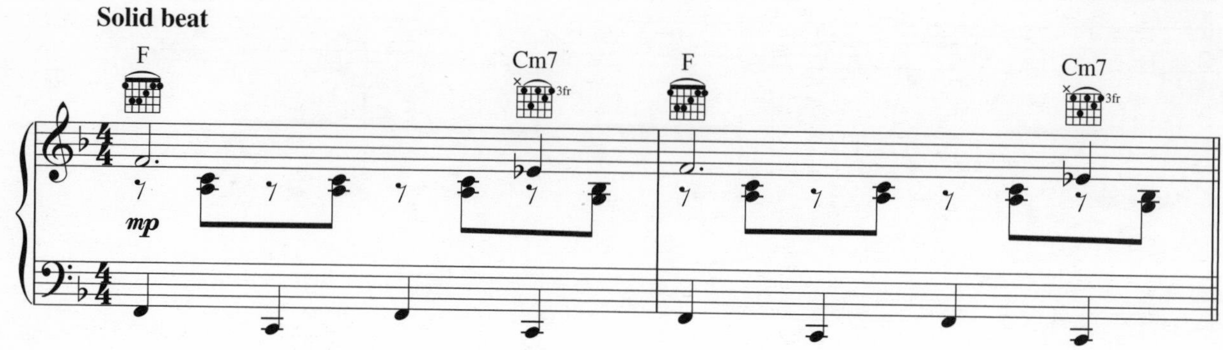

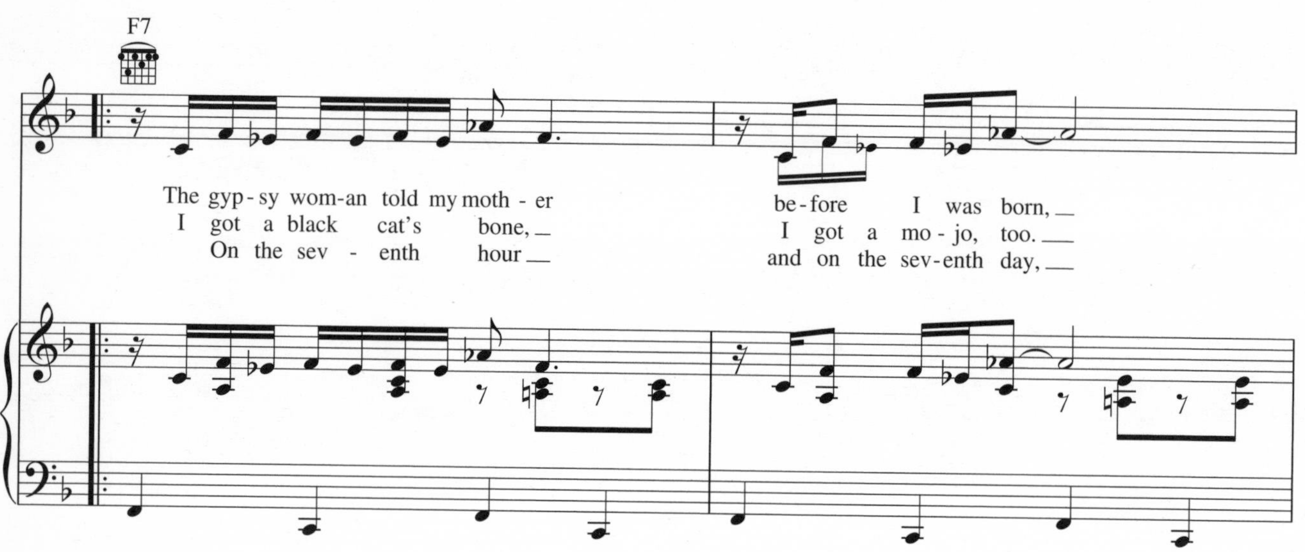

He's gon - na make pret - ty wom - en, he's gon - na make'em jump and shout.
I'm gon - na make you pret - ty girls lead me by the hand.
"He was born for good luck, and that you're gon - na see."

Then the world could know what this was all a - bout."
Then the world will know I'm the hoo-chie coo-chie man.
I've got sev-en hun-dred dol-lars, ba - by, don't you mess with me.
Lord, I'm

B♭9
here, oh yeah, ev - 'ry - bod - y knows I'm

F
here, oh Lord, 'cause I'm a
C7
hoo - chie coo - chie man.
B♭7
Ev - 'ry - bod - y knows I'm
3
1, 2
F
Cm7
F
Cm7
here.
3
F
Cm7
F9
here.
rall.

ICE CREAM MAN

Words and Music by
JOHN BRIM

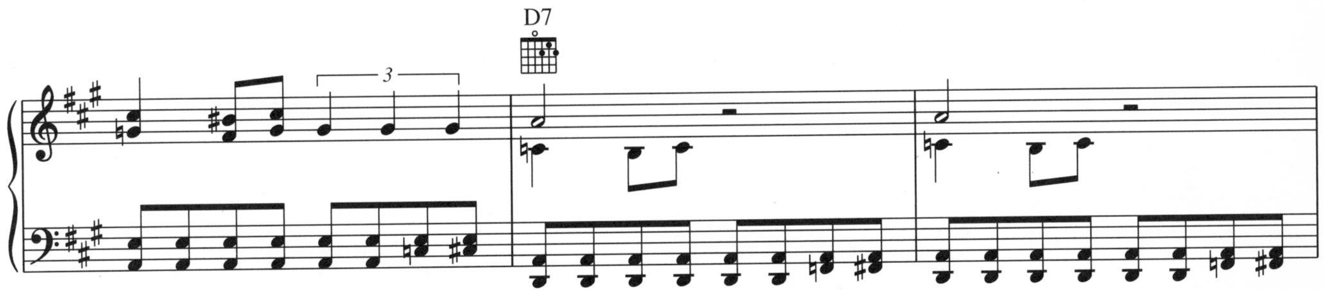

A7
1. Sum-mer-time is here, need some-thin' to keep you cool.
2. (See additional lyrics)
D7
Now, sum-mer-time is here, need some-thin' to keep you cool.
A7
E7
Hey, lit - tle girl,
D7
A7
I've got some - thin' for you.
I'm your ice

D7
A7
cream man,
stop me when I'm pass - in' by.
D7
I'm your ice cream man,
stop me when I'm pass - in' by.
A7
E7
I'll
cool you off, lit - tle girl,
I
D7
To Coda
A7
E7
guar - an - tee I'll sat - is - fy.

A7
I got cream sand-wich-es, dix - ie cups, pop - si-cles, and push - up's, too. I'm your
D7
A7
ice cream man, stop me when I'm pass - in' by.
E7
D7
I'll cool you off, lit-tle girl, I guar-an-tee I'll sat - is - fy.
A7
E7
A7

Additional Lyrics

2. I usually come along just about eleven o'clock.
I usually come along just about eleven o'clock.
Now, if you let me cool you off this time,
You'll be my regular stop.

I got all flavors, including pineapple, too.
I got all flavors, including pineapple, too.
Now, one of my flavors, little girl,
Has gotta be just right for you.

IF YOU LOVE ME LIKE YOU SAY

Words and Music by
LITTLE JOHNNY TAYLOR

C7
why you treat me like you do?
G7
F♯7
F7
Well, I ain't no fool.
I'm cool, I know the
C7
To Coda
N.C.
C7
rule.
Said you'd nev - er run a - round.
Instrumental solo
Said you'd nev - er stay out late.

F7
Said you'd nev - er run a - round, ba - by.
C7
Said you'd nev - er stay out late.
G7
F♯7
F7
Let me tell you, pret - ty babe, I've got to set you
C7
straight.
Solo ends
1
N.C.
If you love me like you
2
N.C.
D.S. al Coda
If you love me like you

CODA
N.C.
G7
F♯7
Why, yah, yah, yah.
F7
C7
I'm cool, I know the rule.
N.C.
G7
F♯7
Why, yah, yah, yah,
F7
C7
N.C.
C7
I'm cool, I know the rule,
yeah!

IT HURTS ME TOO

Words and Music by
MEL LONDON

F7
hind him and you take this mess, When things go
C
G7
C
C7
F
Fm
wrong, go wrong with you, It Hurts Me Too.
C
G+7
C
He loves an-oth-er wom-an and I love you, But you love
F7
C
him and stick to him like glue, When things go wrong, go wrong with

C7
C
C7
F
Fm
C
G+7
C
you, It Hurts Me Too. He bet - ter
leave you, or you got - ta put him down, be - cause I won't
F7
C
stay to see you pushed a - round, when things go wrong, go wrong with
G7
C
C7
F
Fm
C
B
C
you, It Hurts Me Too.

KANSAS CITY

Words and Music by JERRY LEIBER and MIKE STOLLER

G7
F7
crazy way of lovin' there and I'm gonna get me some.
C7
I'm gonna be
C
standin' on the corner
pack my clothes,
Twelfth Street and Vine.
leave at the crack of dawn.
I'm gonna be
I'm goin' to

F7
stand - in' on the cor - ner Twelfth Street and Vine,
pack my clothes, leave at the crack of dawn.
C
with my
My old
G7
F7
Kan - sas Cit - y ba - by and a bot - tle of Kan - sas Cit - y wine.
la - dy will be sleep - in' an' she won't know where I'm gone.
3
C7
Well, I
'Cause if I

C F7

might take a train, I might take a plane, but
stay with that wom - an I know I'm gon - na die, got - ta

C

if I have to walk I'm goin' just the same. I'm go - in' to
find a brand - new ba - by and that's the rea - son why I'm go - in' to

F7

Kan - sas Cit - y, Kan - sas Cit - y here I

C

come. They got a

G7
F7
cra - zy way of lov - in' there and I'm gon - na get me some.
C7
1
I'm go - in' to
2
G7
They got a cra - zy way of lov - in' there and
F7
C7
I'm gon - na get me some.

IT SERVES ME RIGHT TO SUFFER

Words and Music by
JOHN LEE HOOKER

Additional Lyrics

2. Every time I see a woman, and folks, she make me think of mine,
Every time I see a woman, and folks, she make me think of mine,
And that's why and that's why, and folks, I just can't keep 'em cryin'.

3. My doctor put me on milk cream and alcohol,
My doctor put me on milk cream and alcohol,
And so you can just sleep at night.

IT'S MY OWN FAULT DARLIN'

Words and Music by B.B. KING
and JULES BIHARI

Additional Lyrics

2. You used to make your own paychecks, baby,
   And bring them all home to me.
   I'd go out on the hillside, you know,
   And make every woman look and see.

   It's my own fault, baby.
   Treat me the way you wanna do.
   Yes, 'bout the time you was lovin' me, baby,
   At that time, little girl, I didn't love you.

3. Yes, you used to be here with me, baby,
   But now you're runnin' around with the boys.
   You said you was gonna leave me,
   You gonna be o'er in Illinois.

   It's my own fault, baby,
   Treat me the way you wanna do.
   Yes, when you were loving me, woman,
   At that time, little girl, I wouldn't be true.

4. Yes, I fall on my knees,
   Raise up my right hand.
   Yes, I would do better, baby,
   But I just don't understand.

   It's my own fault, baby,
   Treat me the way you wanna do.
   Yes, 'bout the time you were lovin' me, woman,
   At that time, little girl, I wouldn't be true.

KEY TO THE HIGHWAY

Words and Music by BIG BILL BROONZY
and CHAS. SEGAR

Additional Lyrics

2. I'm goin' back to the border
Where I'm better known.
Though you haven't done nothin',
Drove a good man away from home.

3. Oh, gimme one more kiss, mama,
Just before I go,
'Cause when I leave this time,
I won't be back no more.

4. *Repeat Verse 1*

KIDNEY STEW BLUES

Words and Music by LEONA BLACKMAN
and EDDIE VINSON

Moderately

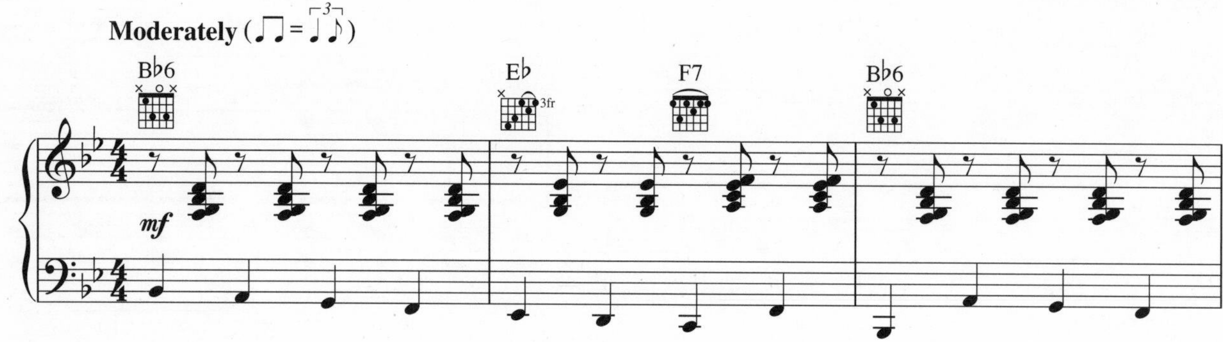

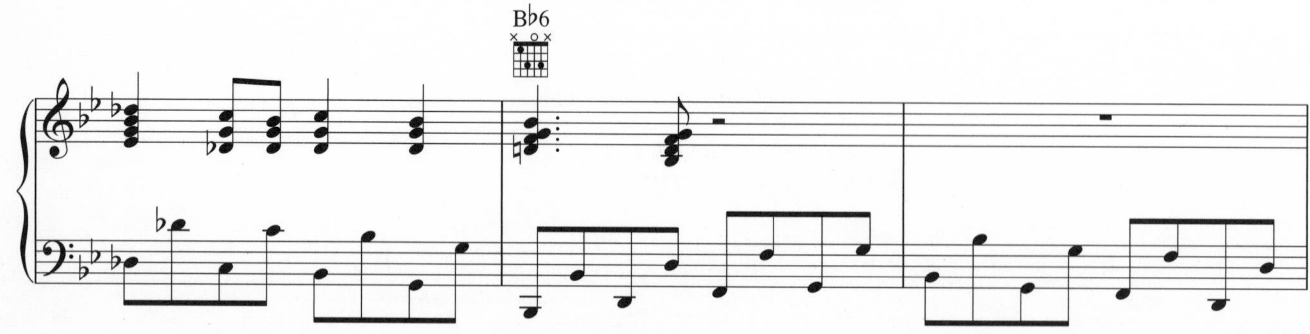

E♭7
B♭6
To Coda
Cra - zy 'bout you, ba - by, but I just ain't got the price.
Go - in' back home and get my ol' gal Sue.
Instrumental solo
E♭7
Cra - zy 'bout you, ba - by,
Go - in' back home
B♭6
but I just ain't got the price.
and get my ol' gal Sue.

F7
You're a high - class ma - ma,
She ain't the cav - i - ar kind,
B♭6
so I guess it ain't no dice.
just plain ol' kid - ney stew.
1, 2
3
Old kid - ney stew,
old kid - ney stew is fine.
Old

E♭7
B♭6
kid - ney stew,
old kid - ney stew is fine.
F7
You can save your mon - ey and keep your peace of
B♭6
D.S. al Coda
mind.
CODA
B♭6
B♭9(add13)

KILLING FLOOR

Words and Music by
CHESTER BURNETT

B♭
quit you
fol - low
went on
knows,
a long time ____ a - go, ___
my first ____ mind ____
when my friend come from ____
Mexico with me,
E♭7
I should - a quit you, ba - by,
if I had to fol - low
I should - a went on
Lord knows,
B♭
long time a - go;
my first mind,
when my friend come from Mexico with me,
I should - a been gone,
I should-a
I'd - a
but now I threw in
and I wouldn't

F7
Eb7
quit you
been gone
with you, baby
have been here.
and went off to Mexi-
it's my second
I let you quit jobbin' killing
Now I'm killing
1-3
Bb
F7
4
co.
time.
floor.
If I had to
I should-a
Lord
floor.
Eb7
Bb
Repeat and Fade

KIND HEARTED WOMAN BLUES

Words and Music by
ROBERT JOHNSON

G7
F7
To Coda
But these e - vil - heart - ed wom - en,
I real - ly love that wom - an,
You well's to kill me
man, they will not let me
can't stand to leave her
as to have it on your
C7
C6
C+
1
G7
be.
be.
2
G7
C7
F7
There ain't but the one thing makes Mis - ter John - son drink, it's
Guitar solo ad lib.
C7
F7
C7
B7
C7
worry'n 'bout how you treat me, ba - by. I be - gan to think, oh,

F7
C7
B7
babe, my life don't feel the same.
C7
G7
F7
You break my heart, when you call mis - ter so and so's
C7
C6
C+
1
G7
name.
2
G7
D.S. al Coda
She's a
CODA
C
C7
C6
C+
G7
C7
mind.

LET ME LOVE YOU BABY

Words and Music by
WILLIE DIXON

G7
ooh wee, ba - by, I de - clare you sure look fine.
ba - by, when you walk, you know you shake like a wil - low tree.
all I own just for a lit - tle bit of your love.
Well, now,
Now,
I'll give you
C7
ooh wee, ba - by, I de - clare you sure look fine.
ba - by, when you walk, you know you shake like a wil - low tree.
all I own just for a lit - tle bit of your love.
G7
Well, now a
A lit - tle
Since I

D7
C7
girl like you make a man - y men change their mind.
girl like you would love to make a fool of me.
met you, ba - by, that's all I been liv - in' for.
G7
1
D7
2
D7
Now,
Let me
G7
love you, ba - by.
Let me love you, ba - by.
C7
Whoa, let me love you, ba - by.

G7
Yes, let me love you, ba - by.
3
D7
Let me love you, ba - by, till your
C7
G7
To Coda
good love drives me cra - zy.
D7
D.S. al Coda
(take 2nd ending)
I'll give you
CODA
G7
N.C.
G7
- zy.

LET THE GOOD TIMES ROLL

Words and Music by SAM THEARD
and FLEECIE MOORE

A♭9
4fr
E♭
3fr
good times roll, let the good times roll.
Fm7
B♭7
3
Don't care if you're young or old.
Fm7
B♭9
B♭7♯5
6fr
E♭
3fr
Get to-geth-er, let the good times roll.
Don't sit there a-mum-blin', and talk-in' trash. If you

E♭7
wan - na have a ball you got - ta spend some cash. Let the
A♭9
4fr
E♭
3fr
good times roll, let the good times roll.
Fm7
B♭7
Fm7
B♭9
B♭7♯5
6fr
Don't care if you're young or old. Get to-geth-er, let the good times
1
E♭
3fr
roll.
2
E♭
3fr
E♭9
roll.

LONESOME WHISTLE BLUES

Words and Music by ALAN MOORE,
ELSON TEAT and RUDY TOOMBS

G7
F7
C7
Wooh
G7
C7
F7
My girl-friend left me, can't e-ven tell me the rea-son
long a-bout mid-night when I heard that old lone - some Can-non -
find you, ba-by, if it takes my whole life to track you
C7
F7
why. Woah, my girl-friend left me,
ball, woah, a - long a - bout mid-night
down. I'm gon - na find you, ba-by,
C7
can't e - ven tell me the rea - son why.
when I heard that old lone - some Can - non - ball,
if it takes my whole life to track you down.

G7
Woah, if I did - n't please you, ba - by,
woah, when I think a - bout you, ba - by,
Woah, if I don't find you by plane,
F7
C7
To Coda
1
G7
ain't be-cause I did - n't try.
tears be - gin to fall.
I'm gon - na use my old blood hound.
Woah, a -
2
G7
C7
Wooh
F7
Wooh

C7
G7
F7
C7
Wooh
G7
D.S. al Coda
I'm gon - na
CODA
G7
C7
F7
C7
Wooh

F7
Wooh
C7
G7
Wooh
F7
Repeat and Fade
C7
G7
Optional Ending
N.C.
D♭9
C9

LITTLE RED ROOSTER

Written by
WILLIE DIXON

1.
2.
G
G
way. The he keeps all the hens
prowl. I tell you that see my red roost-er,
C7
G
G7
C7
fight-ing a-mong them-selves, Tell you that he keeps all the hens
please send him home, Said if you see my red roost-er,
G
D7
fight-ing a-mong them-selves. He don't want no hens in the barn-yard
please send him home. I had no peace in the barn-yard
C7
G
1.
2.
G7
lay-ing eggs for no-bod-y else. Now if you
since the red roost-er's been gone.

LOVE IN VAIN BLUES

Words and Music by
ROBERT JOHNSON

G7
D7/A
with a suit - case in my hand.
G
Am
D7/F♯
Well, it's hard to tell, it's hard to tell when all your love's in vain.
G
G/F
C/E
Cm/E♭
3fr
G/D
D7
All my love's in vain.
G
When the train rolled up to the
G7
sta - tion
I looked her in the eye,

C
when the train rolled up to the sta - tion
G7
D7
G
and I looked her in the eye,
well, I was
Am
D7/F♯
G
G/F
C/E
Cm/E♭
G/D
lone-some, I felt so lone-some
and I could not help but cry.
All my love's in vain.
D7
G
G7
When the train, it left the sta - tion

with two lights on be - hind,
when the train,
C
it left the sta - tion
with two lights on be - hind,
G7
D7
G
Am
well, the blue light was my blues
D7/F♯
G
G/F
C/E
Cm/E♭
G/D
D7/F♯
3fr
and the red light was my mind.
All my love's in vain.
Ooh,

G
G7
hoo, hoo, Wil - lie Mae.
C/G
Oh, hey, hoo, Wil - lie Mae.
G
D7
G
C/G
G
Am
Ooh hoo,
D7/F♯
G
G/F
C/E
Cm/E♭
3fr
G/D
D7/F♯
G
hoo, wee, oh woe, all my love's in vain.

MATCHBOX

Words and Music by
CARL LEE PERKINS

To Coda
E7
D7
A
ain't got no match - es, but I sure got a long way to go.
E7
A
I'm an ol' poor boy and I'm a long way from home;
D7
I'm an ol' poor boy and I'm a
A
long way from home;
I'll

E7
D7
A
never be happy, 'cause ev'rything I ever did was wrong.
E7
A
Well, if you don't want my peaches, honey, please don't shake my
tree;
D7
If you don't want any of those peaches, honey,
A
please don't mess around my tree.
I got news

E7
D7
A
for you, ba - by, leave me here in mis - er - y.
(Spoken:) All right!
E7
A
D7
A
E7
D7
A
E7
A
Well, let me be your lit - tle dog till your big dog comes;

D7
Let me be your lit-tle dog
A
till your big dog comes.
And when your
E7
D7
A
big dog gets here, watch how your pup-py dog runs.
E7
D.S. al Coda
Well, I said I'm
CODA
A
A6

MARY HAD A LITTLE LAMB

Written by
BUDDY GUY

Moderately

2
N.C.
A7
Mar - y had a lit - tle lamb,
day
its fleece was white as snow,
and broke the teach - er's rules,
E7
B7
yeah.
yeah.
Ev - 'ry - where that child went
What a time did they have
A7
E7
1
N.C.
you know the lamb was sure to go, yeah.
that day at school.
He fol - lowed her to school one
2
A7
E7
Guitar solo ad lib.

B7
A7
E7
1, 2
3
Tis - ket,
tas - ket,
a green and yel - low bas - ket.
A7
E7
B7
A7
Sent a let - ter to my ba - by,
on my way I passed _

E7
it.
A7
E7
B7
A7
E7♯9
6fr

MESSIN' WITH THE KID

Words and Music by
MEL LONDON

Moderately fast

C7
G7
did.
You can call it what you want, I
F7
1-4
C7
call it mess-in' with the kid.
(2.) You know the
(3.) Instrumental solo
(4.) You can
(5.) We're gon-na
5
N.C.
C7

MOVE IT ON OVER

Words and Music by
HANK WILLIAMS

F
in ______ She changed the lock on our front door, _ now
in ______ She told me not to play a - round _ but
Bb7
my door key don't fit no more _ So get it on o - ver (Move It On O - ver)
I done let the deal go down _ So pack it on o - ver (Move It On O - ver)
F C7 F C7
scoot it on o - ver ___ (Move It On O - ver) Move o - ver skin - ny dog 'cause the fat dog's mov - in' ___
tote it on o - ver ___ (Move It On O - ver) Move o - ver nice dog 'cause a bad dog's mov - in' ___
1 F
in. ______ This
2 F C7 F
in. ______

MY BABE

Written by
WILLIE DIXON

E♭6
G♭dim7
Fdim7
Fm7
mid - night creep - in'. My babe, true lit - tle ba - by is
do so pleas - in'. My babe, true lit - tle ba - by is
E♭6
G♭dim7
Fdim7
Fm7
E♭6
my babe. My babe, I
my babe. My babe, she don't
G♭dim7
Fdim7
Fm7
E♭6
know she loves me, my babe.
stand no fool - in', my babe.
B♭7
Oh, yes, I know she loves me, my babe.
My babe, she don't stand no fool - in', my babe.

E♭6
E♭7
A♭7
4fr
Oh, yes, I know she loves me, she don't do noth - in' but
Oh, yes, she don't stand no fool - in'. When she's hot there
E♭6
G♭dim7
4fr
Fdim7
Fm7
kiss and hug me. My babe, true lit - tle ba - by is
ain't no cool - in'. My babe, true lit - tle ba - by is
1
E♭6
G♭dim7
Fdim7 Fm7
my babe.
2
E♭6
G♭dim7
Fdim7
Fm7
my babe, true lit - tle ba - by is
Repeat and Fade
Optional Ending
E♭6
G♭dim7
Fdim7
Fm7
my babe. True lit - tle ba - by is
E♭6
my babe.
8vb

NOBODY KNOWS YOU WHEN YOU'RE DOWN AND OUT

Words and Music by
JIMMIE COX

F
A7/E
D7
Gm
3 fr
D7/A
just as soon as my dough got low, I could-n't find a friend, no
Gm
3 fr
B♭
Bdim7
F
Cm/E♭
3 fr
D7
place I'd go. If I ev - er get my hands on a dol - lar a - gain, I'm gon-na
G9
G7♭5
C7
F
A7/E
D7
squeeze it and squeeze it till the ea - gle grins. No - bod - y knows you
Gm
3 fr
D7
Gm
3 fr
B♭
Bdim7
F
Cm/E♭
3 fr
D7
G9
when you're down and out. In your pock-et, not one pen-ny and your friends

C7
F
A7/E
D7
you have-n't an - y. And soon as you get on your feet a - gain,
Gm
D7
Gm
D7
Gm
3 fr
B♭
Bdim7
ev - 'ry-bod - y is your long lost friend.
It's might - y strange, with -
F
Cm/E♭
D7
G9
G7♭5
C7
out a doubt, but no - bod - y wants you when you're down and out.
G9
Db9
C9
F6
C7♯5
No - bod - y wants you when you're down and out.
down and out.
8vb

MY FIRST WIFE LEFT ME

Words and Music by
JOHN LEE HOOKER

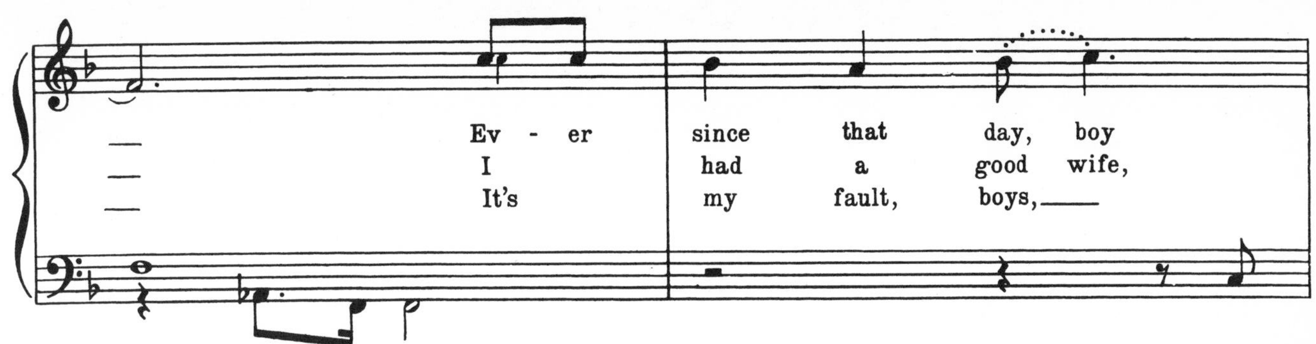

4. She would have been home right now,
   If I hadn't wanted every woman that I'd seen.
   I find one thing,
   These women don't mean you no good.

5. I find out one thing, people,
   These women don't mean you no good.
   You mistreat a good girl for some woman,
   Then she done right turn her back on you.

OH! DARLING

Words and Music by JOHN LENNON
and PAUL McCARTNEY

Slowly

E+ A E

Oh, darling, please believe me,
darling, if you leave me,

mf

F♯m D

I'll never do you no harm; be-
I'll never make it alone; be-

Bm7 E7 Bm7 E7

lieve me when I tell you, I'll never do you no
lieve me when I beg you, don't ever leave me a-

1
A
D
A
E
harm.
Oh,
2
A
D
A
A7
lone.
When you
D
F7
told me
you did-n't need me an-y-more,
well, you
A
know I near-ly broke down
and cried.
When you

B7
told me you did-n't need me an-y-more, well, you
E7
F7♭5
E7
E+
know, I near-ly fell down and died. Oh,
A
E
dar - ling, if you leave me,
dar - ling, please be - lieve me,
F♯m
D
I'll nev - er make it a - lone. Be -
I'll nev - er let you down. (Spoken:) Oh, believe me, darling. Be -

Bm7
E7
1
Bm7
E7
lieve me when I tell you
lieve me when I tell you
I'll nev - er do you no
A
D
A
A7
harm.
(Spoken:) Believe me, darling.
When you
2
Bm7
E7
A
D
A
B♭7
A7
I'll nev - er do you no harm.

PAYING THE COST TO BE THE BOSS

Words and Music by
B.B. KING

G
ba - by, you just got to be out of your mind.
D7
C7
As long as I'm pay - ing the bills, wom - an, I'm pay - ing the
G
D7
cost to be the boss. I'll
G
drink if I want to, and play a lit - tle pok-er, too,
Now that you've got me you act like you're a - shamed,

Don't you say no-thing to me as long as I'm tak-ing care of you.
You don't act like an-y wom-an, you're just us-ing my name.
As long as I'm work-ing, ba-by, and pay-ing all the bills,
I tell you I'm gon-na hand-le all the mon-ey, and I don't want no back talk, —
I don't want no mouth from you a way I'm sup-posed to live.
'Cause if you don't like the way I'm do-ing, just pick up your things and walk,
G7
C7
You must be craz-y, wom-an, you just
You got-ta be craz-y, ba-by, you

G
D7
got - ta be out of your mind.
must be out of your mind.
As long as I'm foot-ing the bills
As long as I'm foot-ing the bills
C7
1
G
and pay - ing the
I'm pay - ing the
cost to be the
D7
boss.
2
G
cost to be the
G9
boss.

PLEASE ACCEPT MY LOVE

Words and Music by B.B. KING
and SAUL BIHARI

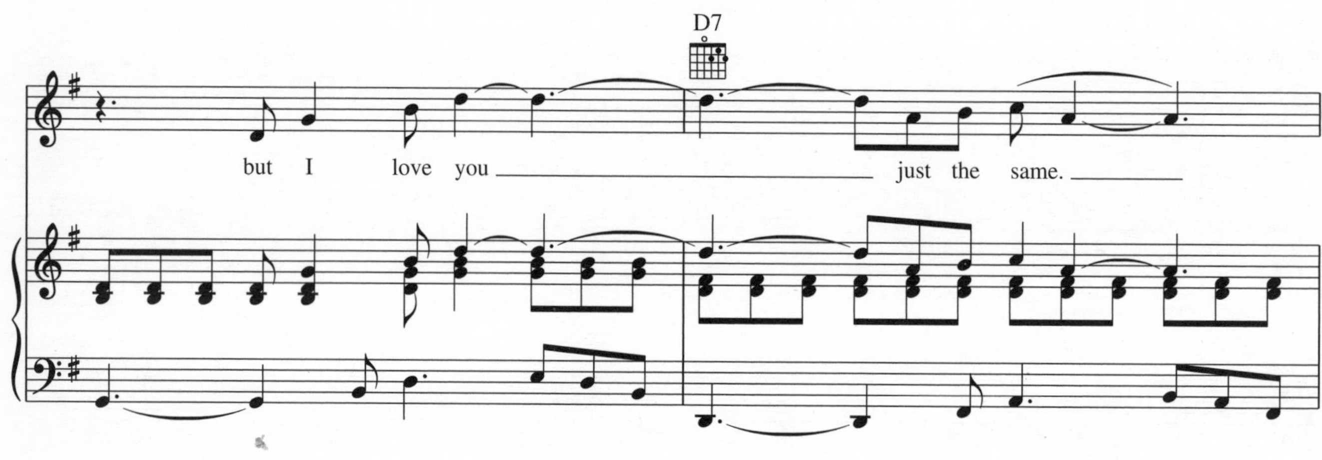

G
till I make you un - der - stand.
N.C.
G
If you on - ly, on - ly knew
just how much I
D7
love you.
Lov - ing you the way
that I do,
you'd take to - night to

G
N.C.
C
love me too.
And like the pic - ture on the wall,
G
please don't let me fall.
It's my
A7
heart
I'm think - in' of,
so won't you
D7
N.C.
D7
N.C.
G
please, please ac - cept my love.
If you let me be your slave,

D7
your love I'll cher-ish to my grave.
And if you die be - fore I do,
1
G
N.C.
I'd end my life to be with you.
And like the pic - ture on the
2
N.C.
G
G7/B
C
C#dim
D7
N.C.
F#7
G7
I'll end my life to be with you.

PRIDE AND JOY

Written by
STEVIE RAY VAUGHAN

B7
A7
E7
B7
E
Well, you've heard a - bout lov - in' giv - in'
love my ba - by with
sight to the blind.
heart and soul.
My ba - by's lov - in' cause the
Love like ours will
A7
sun to shine
nev - er grow old
and she's my sweet lit - tle thing.
She's my

E
B7
pride and joy.
She's my sweet lit - tle ba - by, I'm
A7
E7
1
B7
her lit - tle lov - er boy.
Yeah, I
2
B7
E7
N.C.
E7
N.C.
Yeah, I
love my la - dy, she's long and lean.
love my ba - by like the fin - est wine.
E7
N.C.
E7
You mess with her, you'll see a man get mean.
Stick with her un - til the end of time.
Yes, she's my

A7
E
sweet lit - tle thing.
She's my pride and joy.
B7
A7
She's my sweet lit - tle ba - by, I'm her lit - tle lov - er boy.
E7
To Coda
B7
E7
Guitar solo ad lib.

A7

E7
B7

A7
E7
1
C9
B7

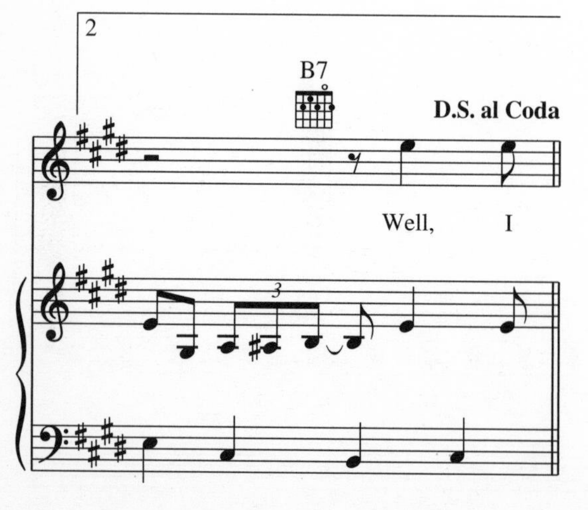
2
B7
D.S. al Coda
Well, I

CODA
B7
E
Yeah, I love my ba-by, my

heart and soul.
Love like ours it won't nev - er grow old.
She's my sweet lit - tle thing.
A7
E
She's my pride and joy.
B7
A7
She's my sweet lit - tle ba - by, I'm her lit - tle lov - er boy.
E7
B7
E7
3

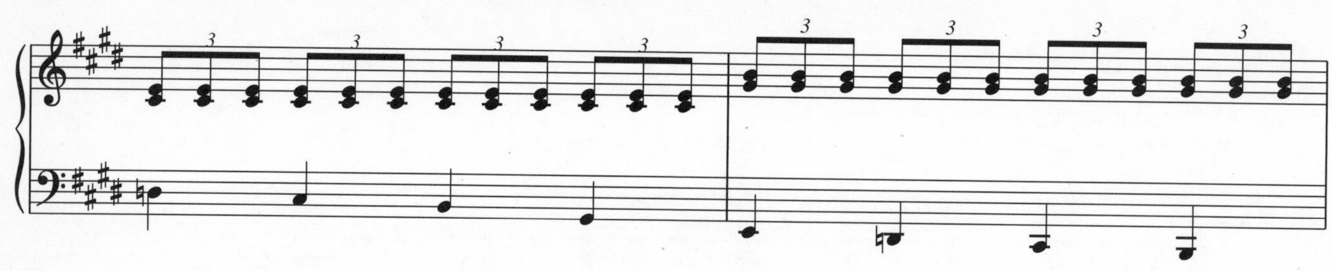

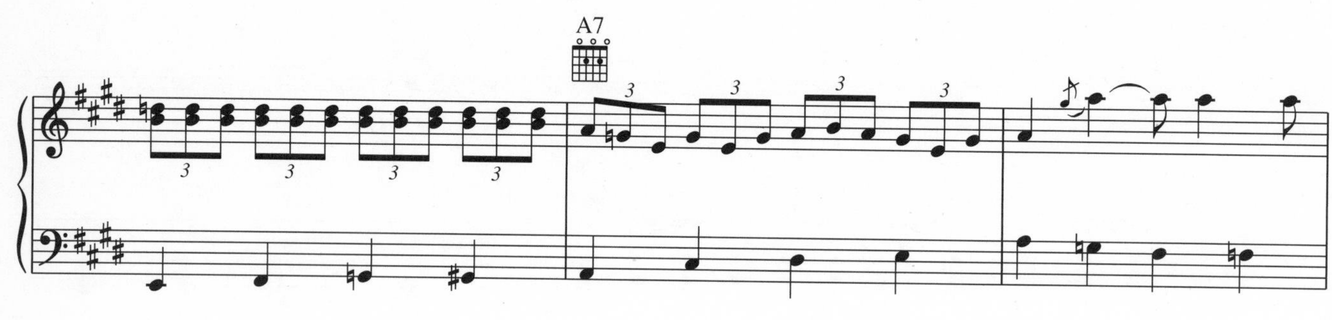
A7

E7
B7

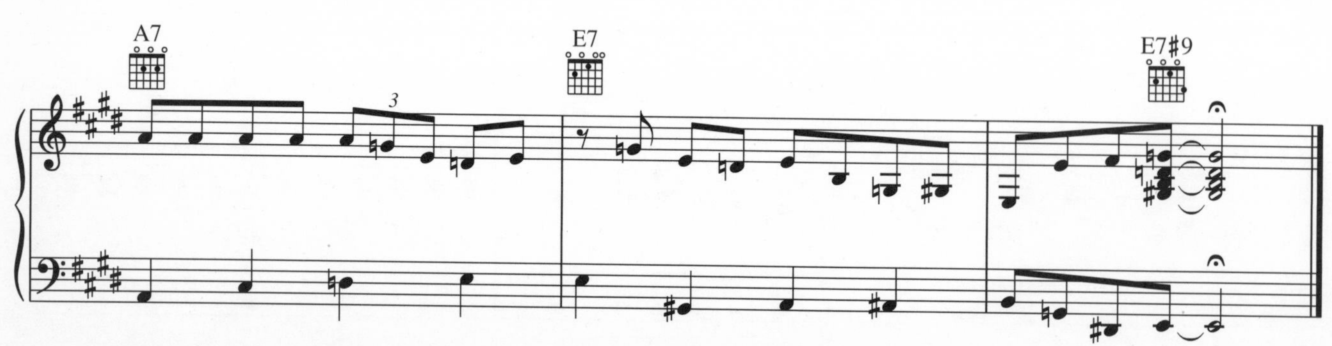
A7
E7
E7#9

SEE SEE RIDER

Words and Music by
MA RAINEY

Dm7
G7
Dm7
G7
C
made me love you. Now your gal has come.
he won't have me, he won't have no gal at all.
D9
4fr
G7
C
G7
C
I'm goin' a - way, ba - by.
See See Rid - er,
G7
C7
I won't be back 'til fall. Law'd Law'd Law'd,
where did you stay last night? Law'd Law'd Law'd, your
F
F♯dim7
C
G+
3fr
G
goin' a - way, ba - by. Won't be back 'til fall.
shoes ain't but - toned, your clothes don't fit you right.

C
C♯dim7
1
Dm7
G7
Dm7
G7
If I find me a good man, won't be back at
You
C
A♭7
G7
2
Dm7
G7
all.
I'm gon - na
did - n't come home 'til the
Dm7
G7
C
G7♯5
C6
sun was shin - ing bright.

RAMBLIN' ON MY MIND

Words and Music by
ROBERT JOHNSON

* Recorded a half step lower.

G
D
Hate to leave my ba - by,
C(add9)
G
G7/F
C/E
E♭+
G/D
but you treats me so un - kind.
I've got mean
things,
I've got mean things all on my mind.
C(add9)
Lit - tle girl, lit - tle girl,
I've got mean things all on my mind.

G
D
Hate to leave you here, babe,
C(add9)
G
G7/F
C/E
E♭+
G/D
but you treats me so un - kind.
Run-nin' down
G
to the sta - tion,
catch the first mail train I see.
A5
B♭5
B5
5fr
(Spoken:) I think I hear her comin' now....
Run-nin' down

C(add9)
G
to the sta - tion,
catch that old first mail train I see.
D
C(add9)
I've got the blues on Miss So - and - So, and the child got the blues a - bout me.
G
G7/F
C/E
Cm/E♭
G/D
G
And I'm leavin' this morn - in'
with my arms fold' up and cryin'.
A5
B♭5
B5
G

C(add9)
And I'm leav-in' this morn-in' with my arms fold' up and cry-in'.
G
I hate to leave
D
my ba - by,
C(add9)
but she treats me so un - kind.
G/D
G7/F
C/E
E♭+
G/D
I've got mean things,
G
I've got mean things on my mind.

C(add9)
I've got mean things, I've got mean things all on my mind.
G
D
I got to leave my ba - by, well,
C(add9)
G
G7/F
C/E
E♭+
G/D
G
she treats me so un - kind.

RECONSIDER BABY

Words and Music by
LOWELL FULSON

G
C7
So long, oh, how I hate to see you
Instrumental ad lib.
G
C7
go. So long,
G
oh, how I hate to see you go. And the
D7
G
way that I will miss you, I guess you will nev - er know.

We've been to - geth - er so long,
Instrumental continues
once did love me,
C7
G
3
to have to sep - a - rate this way.
but now I guess you have changed your mind.
C7
We've been to - geth - er so long,
You said you once did love me,
G
to have to sep - a - rate this way.
but now I guess you have changed your mind.

D7
To Coda
I'm gon-na let you go a-head on, ba-by,
Why don't you re-con-sid-er, ba-by,
G
pray that you'll come back home some-day.
1
D7
2
D7
D.S. al Coda
End instrumental
You said you
CODA
D7
G
G/B
C
Cdim7
D7
A♭9
G9
4fr
give your-self just a lit-tle more time.

ROCK ME BABY

Words and Music by B.B. KING
and JOE BIHARI

rock me all __ night long. ___
like you roll __ a wa-gon wheel._
hon-ey, rock_ me slow. ___
F7
C7
Rock me, ba - by, hon-ey rock me all night long._
Want you to roll me, ba-by, like you roll a wa - gon wheel._
Hey rock me, pret-ty ba-by, ba-by, rock me___ slow._
G7
F7
I want you to rock me, ba-by, like my back ain't got no___
Want you to roll me, ba-by, you don't know how it makes me
Will you rock me, ba-by, 'til I want no
C7
1,2
G7
A♭7
G7
3
G7♯5
C9
bone. ___
feel. ___
more. ___

ROUTE 66

By BOBBY TROUP

F
F13
E♭13
5fr
C13
2fr
F6
B♭9
It winds from Chi - ca - go to L. A.,
F6
B♭9
more than two thou-sand miles all the way.
F6
Gm7
C13
2fr
Get your kicks on Route Six - ty Six!
F
F13
E♭13
5fr
C13
2fr
F/C
B♭9
Now you go thru Saint Loo-ey, Jop - lin, Mis - sou - ri and

F/C
F7
B♭9
O - kla - ho - ma Cit - y is might - y pret - ty. You'll see
Am - a -
F6/9
F
Bdim7
F
Gm7
C7
ril - lo,
Gal - lup, New Mex - i - co,
Flag - staff, Ar - i - zo - na;
Gm7
C7
F6/C
Cdim7
Gm7/C
C7
don't for - get Wi - no - na,
King - man,
Bar - stow,
San Ber - nar - di - no.
Won't
F6
B♭9
F6
you get hip to this time - ly tip:

B♭9
When you make that Cal - i - for - nia trip,
F6
Gm7
C13
get your kicks on Route Six - ty Six!
1
F
D7♭9
C♯7♭9
C7
Gm7/C
2
F
B♭6
Bdim7
F/C
If you
Get your
Gm7
C13
F
E13
F13
kicks on Route Six - ty Six!

THE SKY IS CRYING

By ELMORE JAMES

Slow Blues

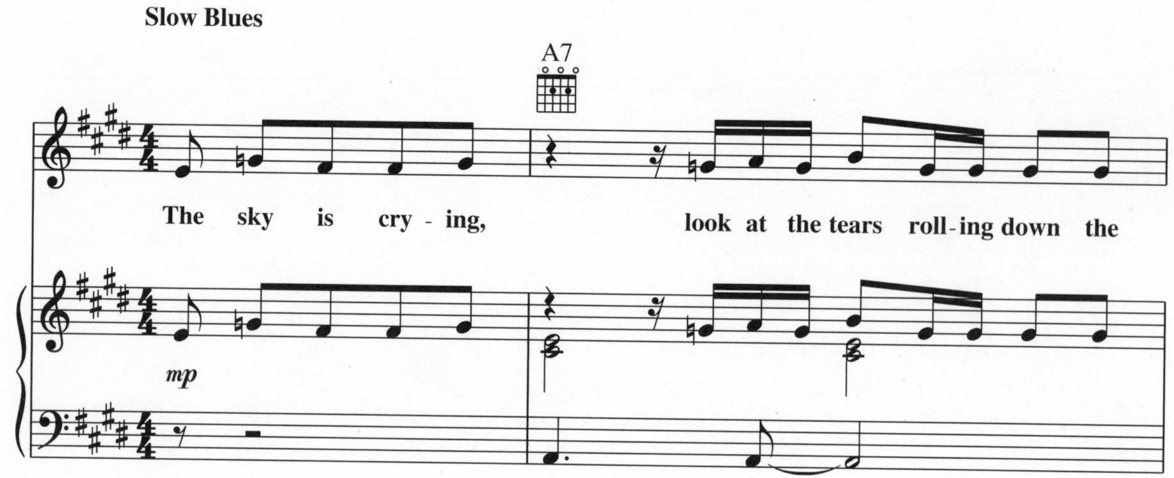

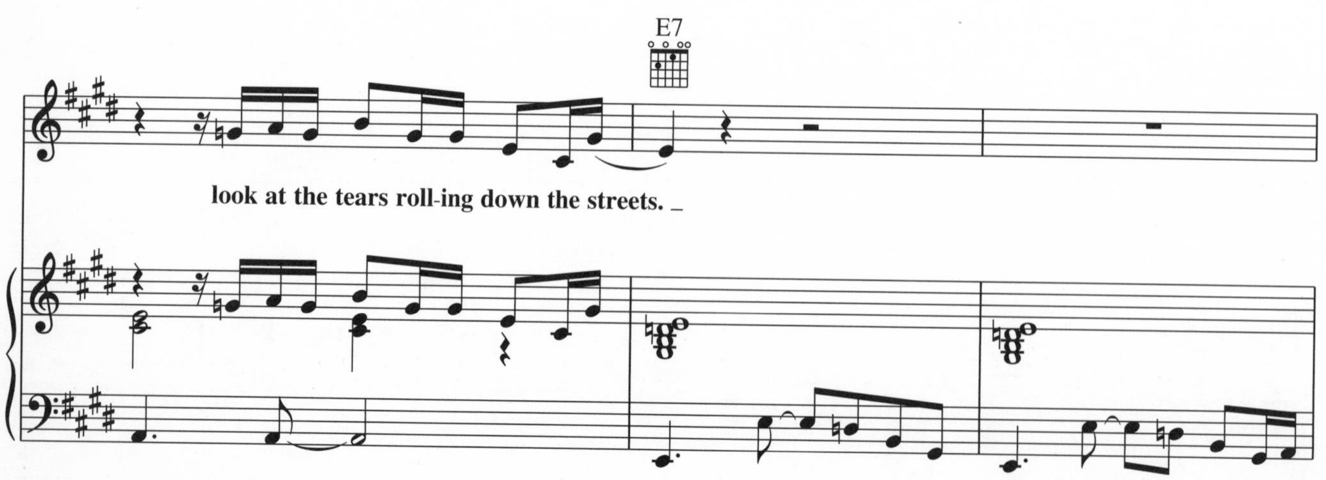

B7
A7
I looked out my win - dow, the rain _ is ___ fall - ing down in
E7
E7
sheets.
My ba - by left me this morn - ing,
A7
E7
Lord knows I don't know the rea - son why;
A7
my ba - by left me this morn - ing, _

E7
I don't know the rea - son why.
B7
And ev - 'ry time I think a - bout it,
A7
E7
I hang my head and cry.
A7
The sun is shin - ing

D7
A7
al-though it's rain-ing in my heart;
D7
the sun is shin - ing al-though it's rain - ing in my
A7
E7
heart.
I love my ba - by,
D7
A7
B♭7
A7
I hate to see us part.
rit.

SMOKESTACK LIGHTNING

Words and Music by
CHESTER BURNETT

hoo,
boo - hoo,
hoo,
boo - hoo,
hoo,
boo - hoo,
boo - hoo?
boo - hoo?
boo - hoo?
1,2
3
Well,
Well,
Well,
Cm
3 fr
stop your train,
let us go for a
fare - thee - well,
nev - er see you no

ride. ___
more. ___
Well, don't you hear me cry - ing, boo -
hoo, ___ boo - hoo, ___
___ boo - hoo? ___
___
1
2
Well, ___ ___

SMOKING GUN

Words and Music by BRUCE BROMBERG,
RICHARD COUSINS and ROBERT CRAY

Moderately

Em

mf

I get a con - stant bus - y sig - nal when I
May - be you want to end ___ it. You've had your
Instrumental solo
stand - ing here ___ be - wil - dered. I can't re -

call you on ___ the phone. ___ I get a strong un - eas - y feel -
fill of my ___ kind of fun. But you don't know how ___ to tell ___
mem - ber just what I've done. ___ I can hear the si - rens whin -

- ing you're not sit - ting there ___ a - lone. ___ I'm hav - in'
___ me, and you know that I'm not that dumb. ___ I put
- ing, my eyes blind - ed by ___ the sun. ___ I

Am7
Em
nas - ty, nas - ty vi - sions and, ba - by, you're in ev - 'ry one,
two and one to - geth - er, and we know that's not an e - ven
know that I'll soon be run - ning, my heart's beat - ing just like a
Am7
yeah. And I'm so a - fraid I'm gon - na find you with a
sum. And I know just where to catch you with that
drum. Now they've knocked me down and tak - en it, that
N.C.
1-4
Em
so - called smok - in' gun.
well - known smok - in' gun.
still hot smok - in' gun.
5
Em
(4.) I'm

Still hot smok - in' gun.
They've tak - en it, that
still hot smok - in' gun.
Optional Ending
Repeat and Fade

SOMEDAY, AFTER AWHILE
(You'll Be Sorry)

Words and Music by FREDDIE KING
and SONNY THOMPSON

G7
G♯dim7
heav - y
with aches and pains.
roll
all those clouds a - way.
know
way down the line
I said, but
D
Bm7
Em7
A7
To Coda
some- day,
some- day, ba - by,
af - ter 'while
you will be
D
D/F♯
G
G♯dim7
1
D
A7
sor - ry.
Ev - 'ry
2
D
D7
G7
Trou - ble, trou - ble,
trou - ble on my

D
mind.
Trou - ble, trou - ble
way down the
E7
line.
I don't need,
I don't need no
A7
D.S. al Coda
sym-pa-thy,
so,
babe,
babe,
don't you,
don't you pit-y me.
CODA
D
D/F♯
G
G♯dim7
D
E♭9
D9
4fr
sor - ry.

STATESBORO BLUES

Words and Music by
WILLY McTELL

D7
A7
G7
D7
A7
D7
G7
Solo ends
1.,4. Wake up, ma - ma,
2.,3. (See additional lyrics)
turn your lamp down low._
D7
G7
Wake up, ma - ma,

D7
turn your lamp down low. Ya
A7
G7
D7
To Coda
got no nerve, ba - by to turn Un-cle John from your door.
1,3
A7
2
A7
D7
Guitar solo
G7
D7

G7 D7

A7 G7

D7 | 1 A7 | 2 A7

Solo ends Well, my

D7 N.C.

ma - ma died and left me, my pa - pa died and left me. I ain't good look-in', ba - by, but I'm

Additional Lyrics

2. I woke up this mornin', and I had them Statesboro blues.
I woke up this mornin', and I had them Statesboro blues.
Well, I looked over in the corner, baby.
Your grandpa seem to have them, too.

3. I love that woman better than any woman I've ever seen.
Well, I love that woman better than any woman I've ever seen.
Well, she treat me like a king, yeah, yeah, yeah.
I treat her like a doggone queen.

(They Call It)
STORMY MONDAY
(Stormy Monday Blues)

Words and Music by
AARON "T-BONE" WALKER

EXTRA LYRICS

2

Yes, the eagle flies on Friday,
And Saturday I go out to play
Eagle flies on Friday,
And Saturday I go out to play..
Sunday I go to church,
Then I kneel down to pray.

3

Lord have mercy,
Lord have mercy on me
Lord have mercy,
My heart's in misery.
Crazy 'bout my baby,
Yes, send her back to me.

STORMY WEATHER
(Keeps Rainin' All the Time)

Lyric by TED KOEHLER
Music by HAROLD ARLEN

Em7
A11
D
Em7
A7♭9
D
Just can't get my poor self to - geth - er,
I'm wea - ry all the time,
the
G
D D♯dim
Em7
A7♭9
D
Em7 D/F♯
G
time,
So wea-ry all the time.
When he went a - way the blues walked
D
G
D
G
D
in and met me.
If he stays a - way old rock - in' chair will get me.
G
D
G
D
B7♭5
All I do is pray the Lord a - bove will let me walk in the sun once

E7
A7♭9
A7
D
D♯dim
Em7
A9
more. Can't go on, ev - 'ry - thing I had is gone, Storm - y
D
Em7
A11
D
Weath - er, Since my man and I ain't to - geth - er,
Em7
A7♭9
D
Em7
A7♭9
keeps rain - in' all the time, keep rain - in' all the
1
Segue to Interlude
D
Bm
D
Bm
D
time.
2
Fine
D
Em7
Dmaj7
G
D
time.
rall.

Interlude
Gm6
Em7♭5
Gm9
D9
I walk a - round, heav - y - heart - ed and sad.
Night comes a - round and I'm
D13
E9
still feel - in' bad.
Rain pour - in' down, blind - in' ev - 'ry hope I had.
This
A
Bm7
Cdim
A7/C♯
Dmaj9/C♯
D6(add2)
pit - ter - in' pat - ter - in' beat - in' an' splat - ter - in' drives me mad,
Love, love,
E13/C♯
E9
A11
A13
D.S. al Fine
love, love,
this mis - er - y is just too much for me.
Can't go

SWEET HOME CHICAGO

Words and Music by
ROBERT JOHNSON

* Recorded a half step lower.

G7
D7/A
go,
3
back to the land of Cal-i-for-nia, to my
G7
G7/D
C♯dim
Cm
G7
D7/A
sweet home, Chi-ca-go?
Oh,
G7
C7
G7
ba-by, don't you want to go,
C7
oh,
ba-by, don't you want to

G7 D7/A

go, back to that land of Cal - i - for - nia, to

G7 G7/D C Cm G7 D7/A

my sweet home, Chi - ca - go? Now,

G7

one and one is two, two and two is four. I'm heav-y load-ed, ba-by. I'm

C7

booked I got-ta go. Cry-in' ba - by, hon - ey, don't you want to

G7
D7/A
go,
back to the land of Cal - i - for - nia, to my
G7/D
C♯dim
Cm
D7/A
sweet home, Chi - ca - go?
Now,
two and two is four, four and two is six. You gon'
keep on mon - keyin' 'round here, friend - boy, you gon' get your busi - ness all in a trick. Well, I'm cry - in',

C7
G7
ba - by,
hon - ey, don't you want to go,
D7/A
G7
back to the land of Cal - i - for - nia,
to my sweet home, Chi - ca - go?
G7/D
C♯dim
Cm
G7
D7/A
G7
Now, six and two is eight,
eight and two is ten.
Friend - boy, she trick you one time, she

C7
sure gon' do it a-gain. And I'm cry-in' hey, ba-by, don't you want to
G7
D7/A
go, to the land of Cal-i-for-nia, to my
G7
G7/D
C♯dim
Cm
4fr
3fr
G7
D7/A
sweet home, Chi-ca-go? I'm
G7
go-in' to Cal-i-for-nia, from Des-and-a-Moines I-o-way.

C7
Some - bod - y will tell me that you need my help some - day. Cryin' hey, hey,
G7
ba - by, don't you want to go, back to the land of
D7/A
G7
Cal - i - for - nia, to my sweet home, Chi - ca - go?
G7/D
G7/F
C/E
Cm/E♭
G7

SWEET SIXTEEN

Words and Music by B.B. KING
and JOE BIHARI

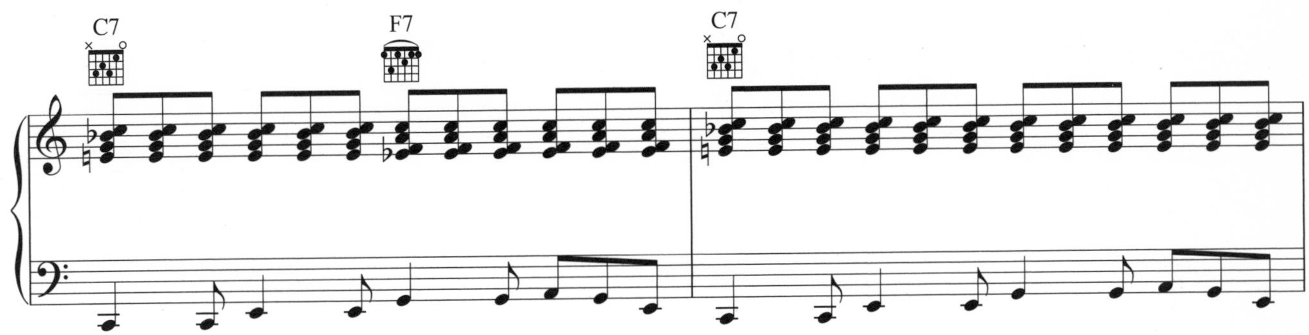

G7
F7
C7
C7/E
F6
F♯dim7
G7
C7
F7
1. When I first met you, ba - by,
2.-6. (See additional lyrics)
ba - by, you were just
sweet six -
C7
teen.

F7
When I first met you, ba - by,
ba - by, you were just sweet six -
C7
F7
C7
teen.
G7
F7
You'd just left your home then, ba - by.
You were the
Last time To Coda
1,2,4,5
C7
C7/E
F6
F♯dim7
G7
sweet - est thing I'd ev - er seen.

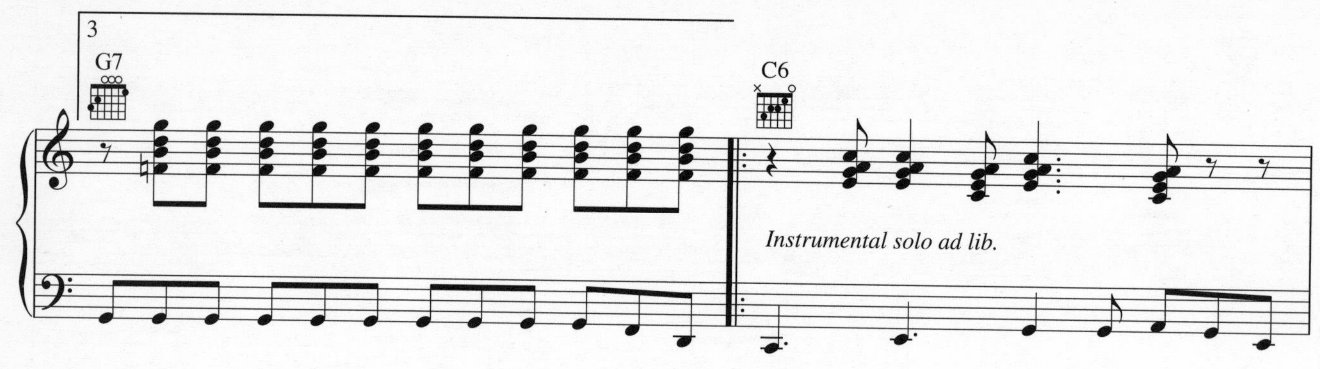
3
G7
C6
Instrumental solo ad lib.

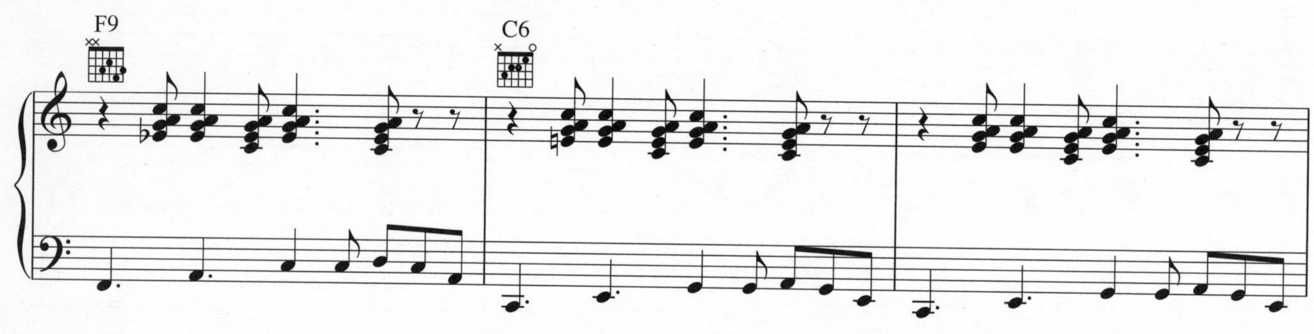
F9
C6

F9
C6

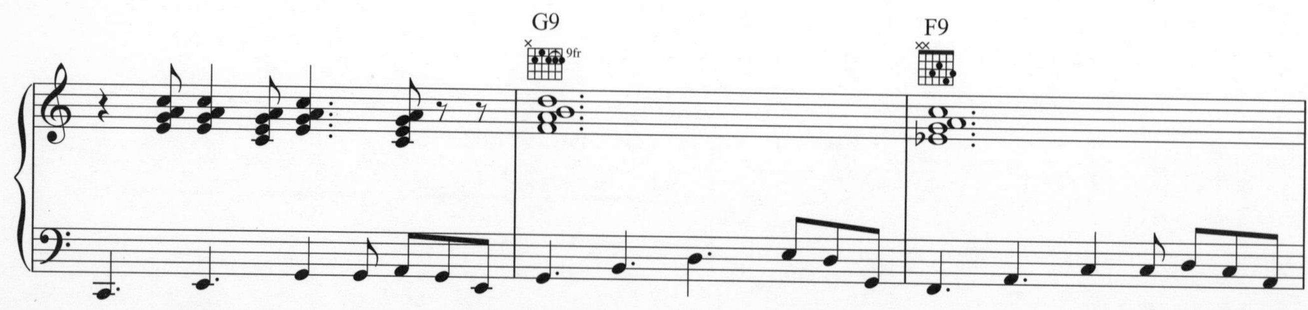
G9
9fr
F9

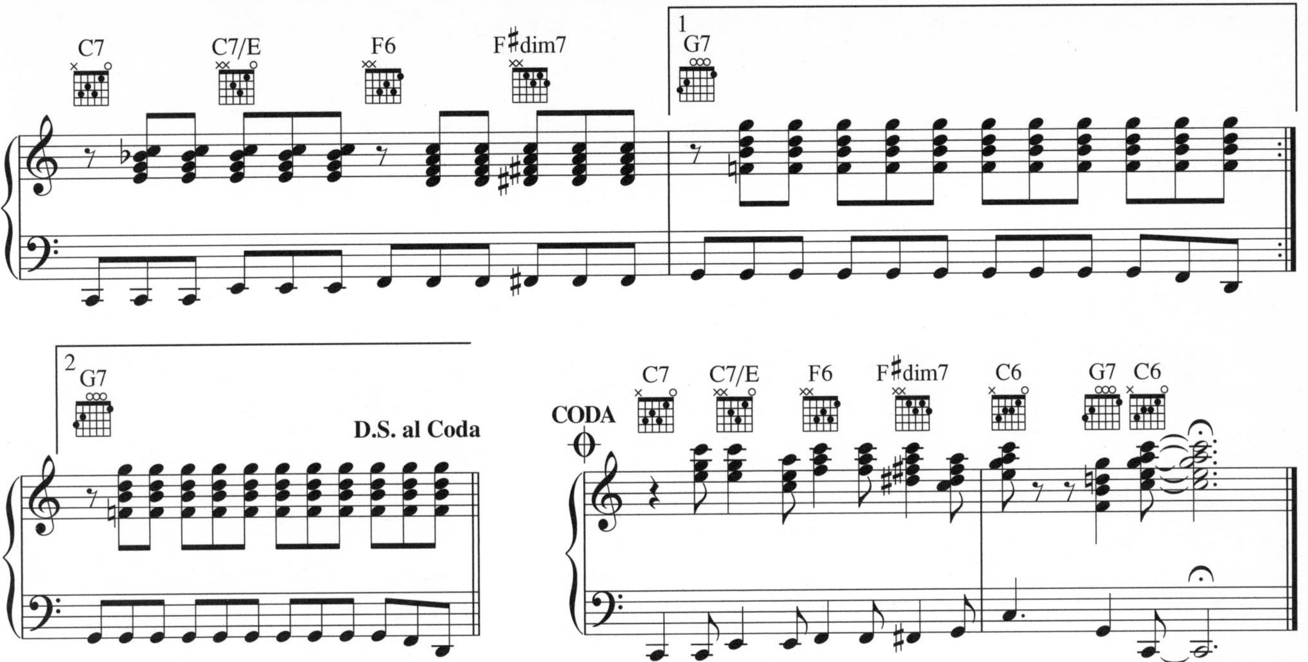

Additional Lyrics

2. But you wouldn't do nothing, baby
You wouldn't do anything I asked to
You wouldn't do nothing for me, baby
You wouldn't do anything I asked to
You know you ran away from your home, baby,
And now you wanna run away from old B., too

3. You know I love you, babe
and I'll do anything you tell me to
You know I love you
and I'll do anything you tell me to
Well, there ain't nothing in the world, woman,
Babe, it ain't nothing,
Nothing in the world I wouldn't do it for you.

4. I just got back from Vietnam, baby,
And you know I'm a long, long way from New Orleans.
I just got back from Vietnam, baby,
And you know I'm a long, long way from New Orleans.
I'm having so much trouble, babe,
I wonder what in the world is gonna happen to me.

5. You can treat me mean, baby,
But I'll keep on loving you just the same.
You can treat me mean, baby,
But I'll keep on loving you just the same.
But one of these days, baby,
You're gonna give a lot of money
To hear someone call my name.

6. Yes, sweet sixteen baby... sweet sixteen...
Yes, the sweetest thing, baby,
The sweetest thing I ever seen.
You know I'm having so much trouble, woman,
Baby, I wonder,
Yes, I wonder,
Baby, I wonder,
Oh, I wonder what in the world's gonna happen to me.

TEXAS FLOOD

Words and Music by LARRY DAVIS
and JOSEPH W. SCOTT

F7
and all the tel - e-phone lines are down.
Man, I'm stand-ing out here in the rain.
Lord, I'm com-ing back home to stay.
Well, I been
Well,
Well, where there's
C7
try - ing to call my ba - by
flood wat - ers keep on roll - ing.
no floods and tor - na - dos.
B♭7
but I can't get a sin - gle
Man, it's a - bout to drive me in -
Ba - by, and the sun shines ev - 'ry
F7
sound.
sane.
day.
1,2
Gm7
C7
Well,
Well,
3
C7♯5
F

THE THINGS THAT I USED TO DO

Words and Music by
EDDIE "GUITAR SLIM" JONES

C9
B♭9
I used to sit and hold your hand, dar - lin',
cry, ___ ba-by, do not go.
F7
C9
2. I used to
F7
B♭9
search all night for you, dar - lin'.
4. (See additional lyrics)
Lord, my search would al-ways end in
4
F7
B♭9
vain.
I used to search all night for you, dar-lin'.

Additional Lyrics

4. I'm goin' to send you back to your mama, darlin'. Lord, I'm goin' back to my family, too.
   I'm goin' to send you back to your mama, darlin'. Lord, I'm goin' back to my family, too.
   Nothin' I can do to please you, darlin'.
   Oh, I just can't get along wit' you.

THREE HOURS PAST MIDNIGHT

Words and Music by JOHNNY WATSON
and SAUL BIHARI

G7
D7
round. _
Well, I lis-ten so hard ___ to hear her foot-steps.
To Coda
C7
G7
C7
1
G7
D7
Ain't ___ e-ven heard _ a sound.
Well, I
2
G7
D7
G7
C7

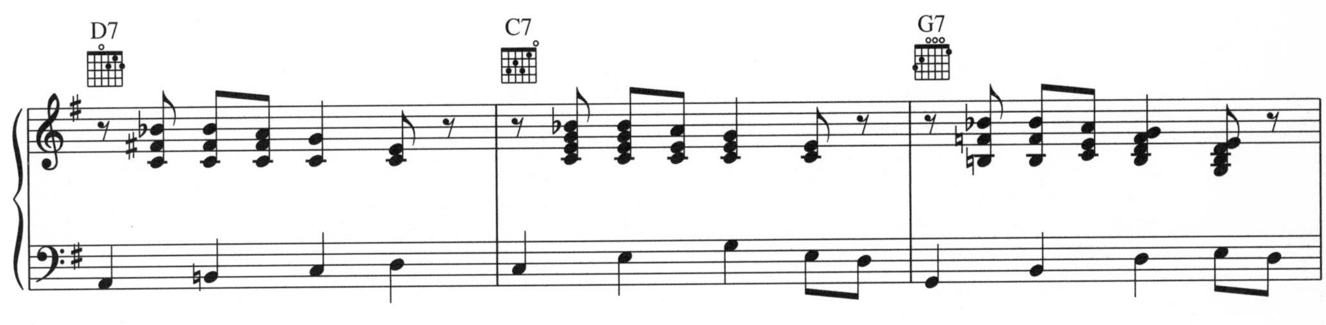

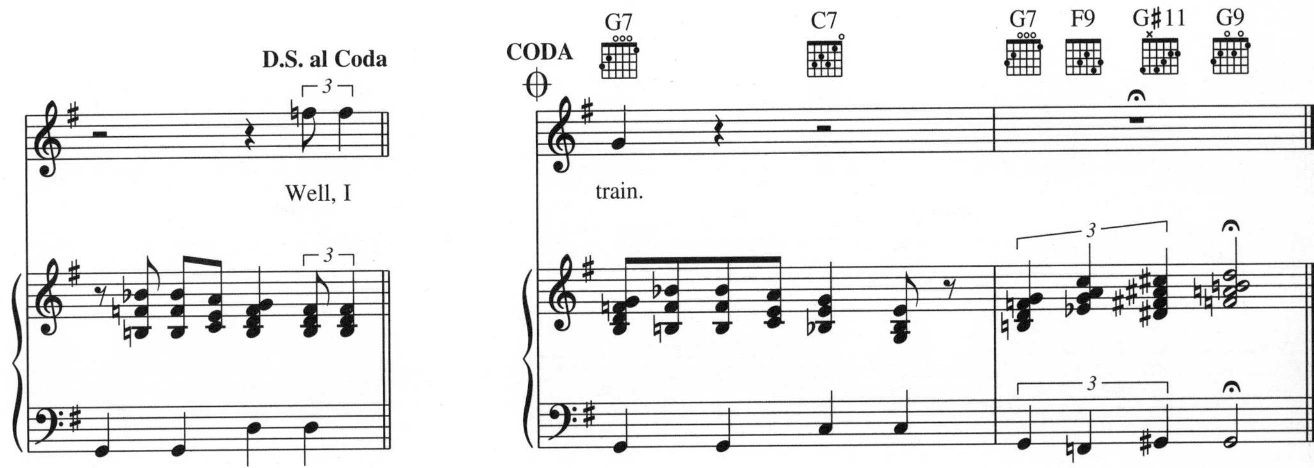

Additional Lyrics

2. Well, I toss and tumble on my pillow, but I just can't close my eyes.
   Well, I toss and tumble on my pillow, but I just can't close my eyes.
   If my baby don't come back pretty soon,
   Yes, I just can't be satisfied.

3. Well, I tried so hard to take it, but my baby's drivin' me insane.
   Well, I tried so hard to take it, but my baby's drivin' me insane.
   Well, if she don't come back pretty soon,
   Yes, gonna catch that midnight train.

THIRD DEGREE

Written by WILLIE DIXON
and EDDIE BOYD

D7
bad luck is kill-in' me.
B♭9
A9
5fr
Well, I just can't stand
G9
9fr
no more of this
1-3
D7
G7
third de-gree.
D7
A7
4
D7
D7/F♯
G7
G♯dim7
D7
E♭9
D9
4fr
third de-gree.

THE THRILL IS GONE

Words and Music by ROY HAWKINS
and RICK DARNELL

G
You know you done me wrong, ba -
Some - day I know I'll be o - pen armed, ba -
F#7sus
F#7
Bm
- by. And you'll be sor - ry some day.
- by, just like I know a good man
F#7
Bm
should.
The thrill is gone.
You know I'm free free now,
It's gone a - way from me.
ba - by. I'm free from your spell.

Em
The thrill is gone, ba - by.
Oh I'm free free free now.
Bm
The thrill has gone a - way from me.
I'm free from your spell.
G
F#7
Al - though I'll still live on, but so
And now that it's all o - ver, all I can
Bm
1
F#7
2
F#7 Bm
lone - ly I'll be.
do is wish you well.

WANG DANG DOODLE

Written by
WILLIE DIXON

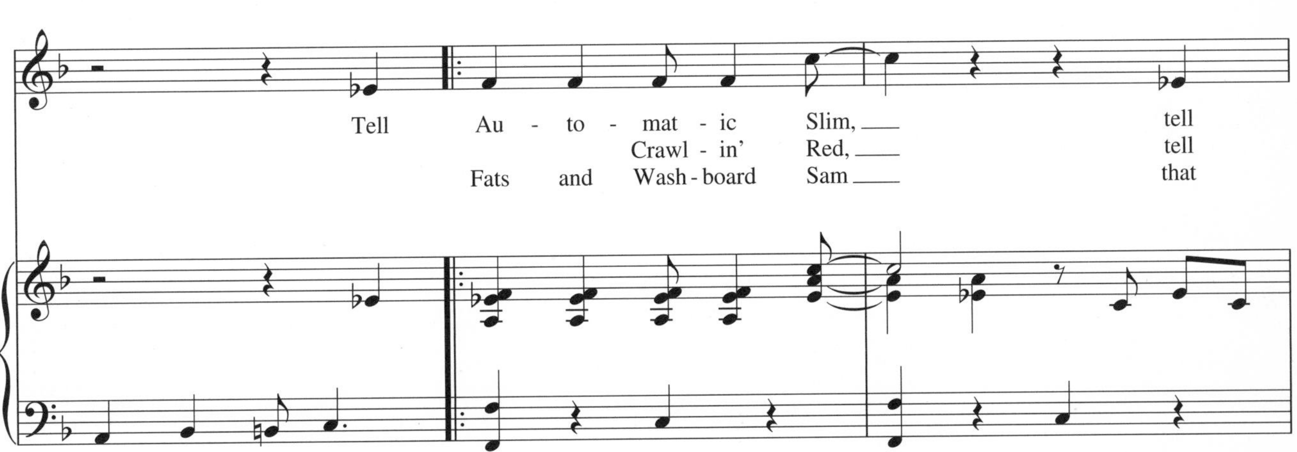

nie, tell Fast Talk-in' Fan - nie.
to tell ev - 'ry - bod - y he meets. To -
we got saw - dust on the flo'. Tell
We gon - na pitch a ball a - down to that un - ion hall.
night we need no rest, we gon - na real - ly throw a mess.
Peg and Car - o - line Din' we gon - na have a heck of a time,
We gon - na romp and tromp till mid - night, we gon - na
We gon - na knock down all the win - dows, we gon - na
and when the fish scent fills the air, there'll be
fuss and fight till day - light.
kick down all the doors.
snuff juice ev - 'ry - where.
We gon - na pitch a Wang Dang

Doo-dle all night long.
All night
long, all night long.
All night
long, all night long. We gon-na pitch a Wang Dang
1, 2
3
Doo-dle all night long.
Tell
Tell

TROUBLE IN MIND

Words and Music by
RICHARD M. JONES

B7
E
my back door some - day.
3
3
3
B7
E
Now all you men's the same,
B7
E7
3
but not a one e - nough to change my
3
3
A7
E
name, 'cause that sun's gon - na shine in

B7
E
my back door some - day.
3
3
3
B7
E
I'm gon - na lay my head
B7
E7
on that lone - some rail - road
A7
E
line, and let the two - nine - teen

B7
E
B7
ease my trou - bled mind.
Trou - ble in
R.H.
E
B7
E7
mind, I'm blue, but I won't be blue al -
A7
E
ways, 'cause that wind's gon - na come and
B7
E
E7
blow my blues a - way.

TUPELO
(Tupelo Blues)

Words and Music by
JOHN LEE HOOKER

NARRATION

Did you read about the flood? It happened long time ago,
A little country town way back in Mississippi.
It rained and it rained, it rained both night and day.
The poor people got worried, they began to cry,
"Lord have mercy, where can we go now?"

There were women and there was children screaming and crying,
"Lord have mercy and a great disaster, who can we turn to now,
but you?"
The great flood of TUPELO, Mississippi.

It Happened one evening, one Friday evening a long time ago,
It rained and it started raining.
The people of TUPELO, out on the farm gathering their harvest,
A dark cloud rolled back in TUPELO, Mississippi. Hm Hm

— It
rained both night and
day, The
poor peo - ple had no place to
go
Hm Hm, In a
lit - tle Town,
called TU - PE -
- LO.
repeat and fade

YOU SHOOK ME

Words and Music by WILLIE DIXON
and J.B. LENOIR

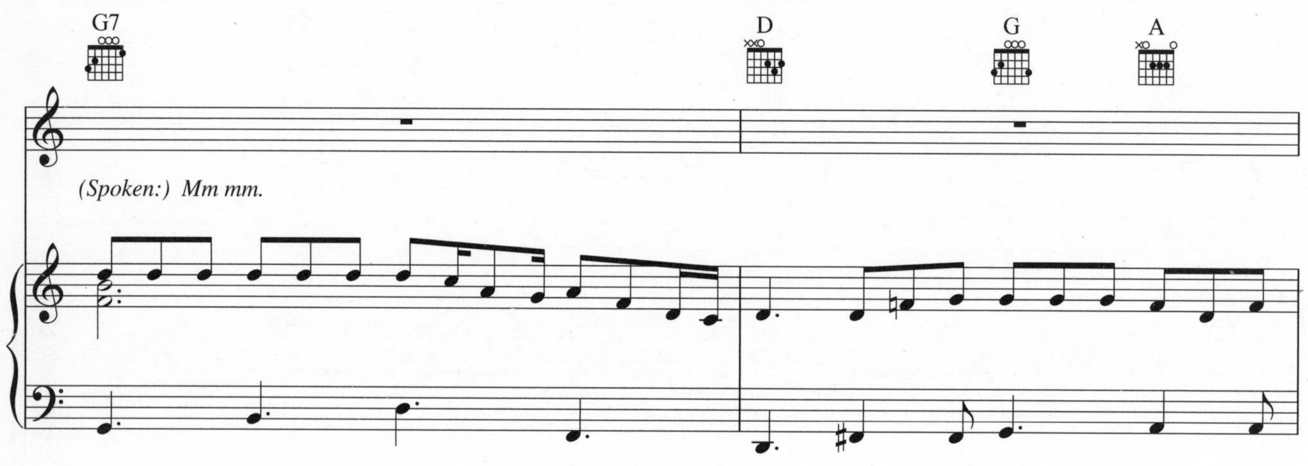

You shook me all night long.
just like a hur - ri - cane.
G7
You know you shook me, ba - by.
You know you move me, ba - by,
D7
You shook me all night long.
just like a hur - ri - cane.
A7
Oh, you kept on shak - ing me, dar - ling.
Oh, you know you move me, dar - ling,

G7
D7
Oh, you messed up my hap - py home.
just like a earth - quake move the land.
1
2
You know you move
Oh,
some time I won - der
what my poor wife and child's gon - na do.
Oh,

G7
some-time I won - der
what my poor wife and child's gon-na do.
D7
Hey,
A7
you knowed you made me mis-treat them, dar - ling.
G7
Whoa, I'm mad-ly in love with you.
D7
A7
D.S. and Fade
You know you shook

YOU UPSET ME BABY

Words and Music by B.B. KING
and JULES BIHARI

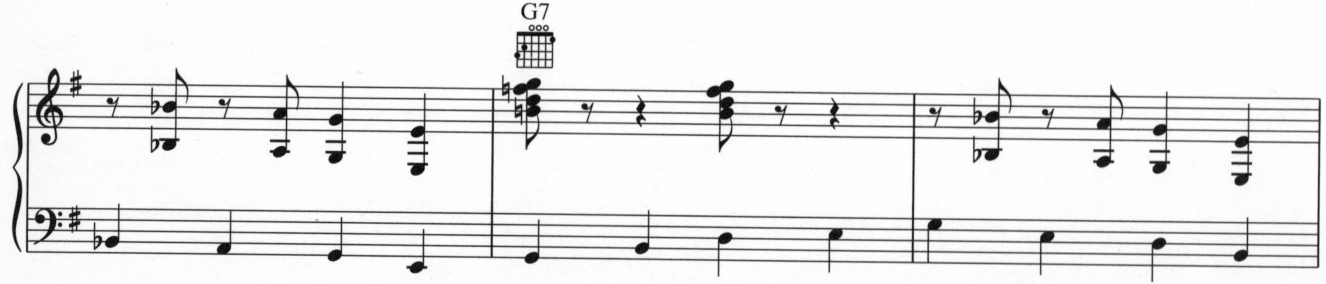

A7
D7
G7
G7
N.C.
Am7
Yeah, she's thir - ty - six in the bust,
not ___ too tall,
(D.S.) tried to de - scribe her,
G7
N.C.
Am7
G7
N.C.
twen - ty - eight in the waist,
com - plex - ion is fair,
it's hard ___ to start.
for - ty - four in the hips, she's got a
man, she knocks ___ me out the way she
I bet - ter stop ___ now be - cause I've
C7
real cra - zy leg. ___
wears _ her hair. ___
got a weak heart. ___
You up - sets me, ba - by,
yes,

G7
D7
you up - sets __ me, ba - by.
(1.) Yes, I'm tell-in' you peo-ple she's some-thin' fine _
(2.,3.,D.S.) Like bein' hit ____ by __ a fall - in' tree, -
C7
1,2
G7
To Coda
that you real - ly ought - a see.
wom - an, what you do to me.
Well, she's
Well, I've
3
G7
do to me.
G7

C7
G7

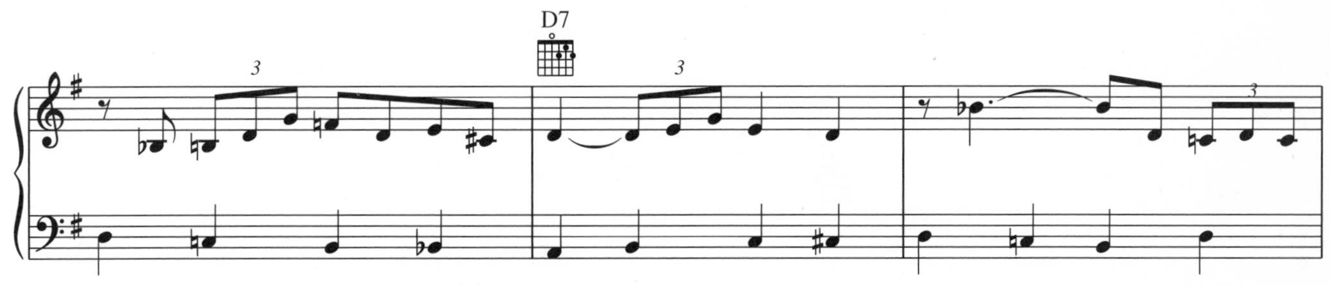
D7
3

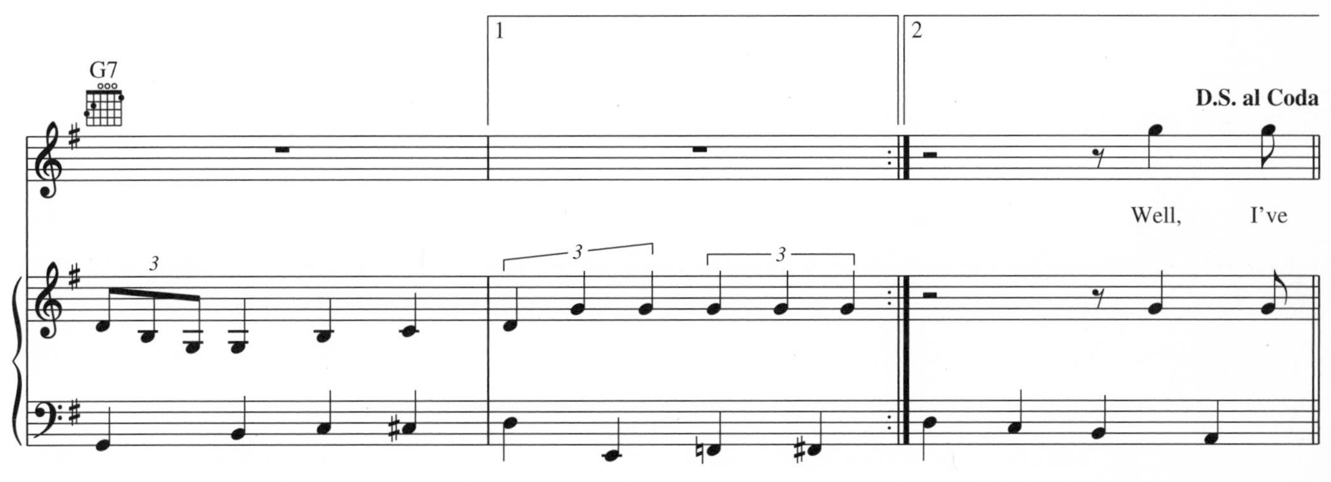
G7
1
2
D.S. al Coda
Well, I've

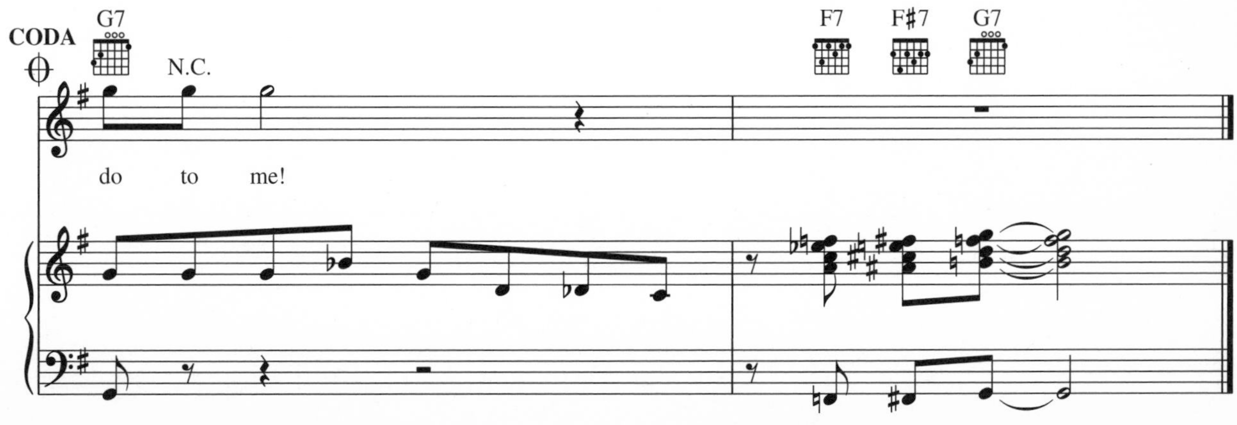
CODA
G7
N.C.
do to me!
F7
F#7
G7

WHY I SING THE BLUES

Words and Music by B.B. KING
and DAVE CLARK

C
first got the blues, they brought me o - ver on a ship.
laid in the ghetto flats; cold and numb. I
stood in line down in the coun - ty hall. I
mp
pp
C7
Men were stand - ing o - ver me and a lot more with the whip, and ev - 'ry -
heard the rats tell the bed - bugs to give the roach - es some, and ev - 'ry -
heard a man say we are go - ing to build some new a - part - ments for y'all
mp
pp
F7
C
bod - y wan - na know
bod - y wan - na know
(and) ev'rybody wan - na know
why I sing the blues.
mp
pp
mp

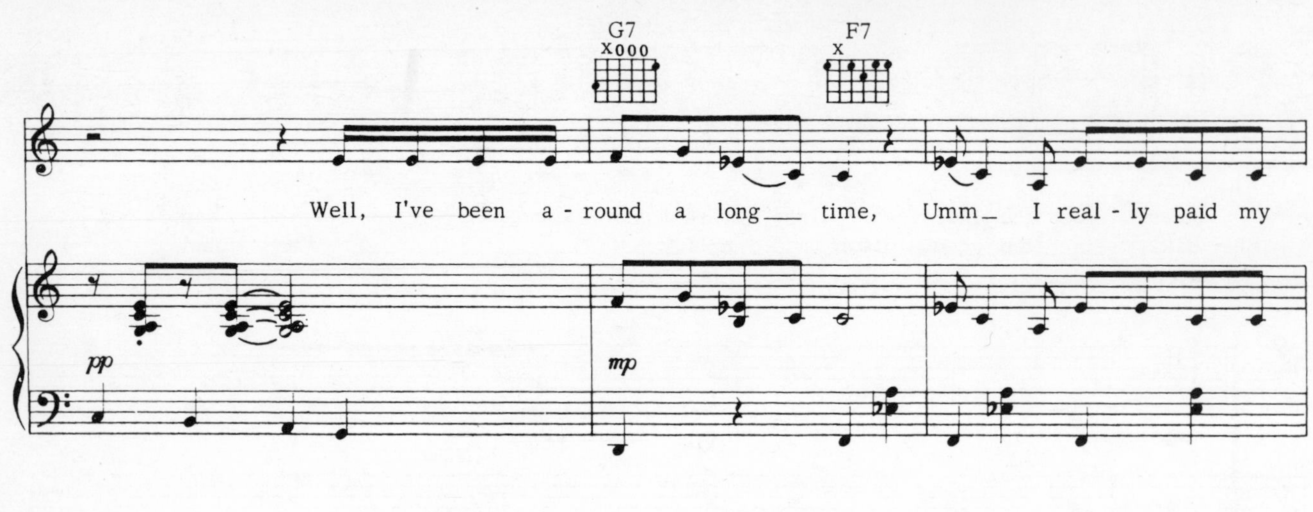

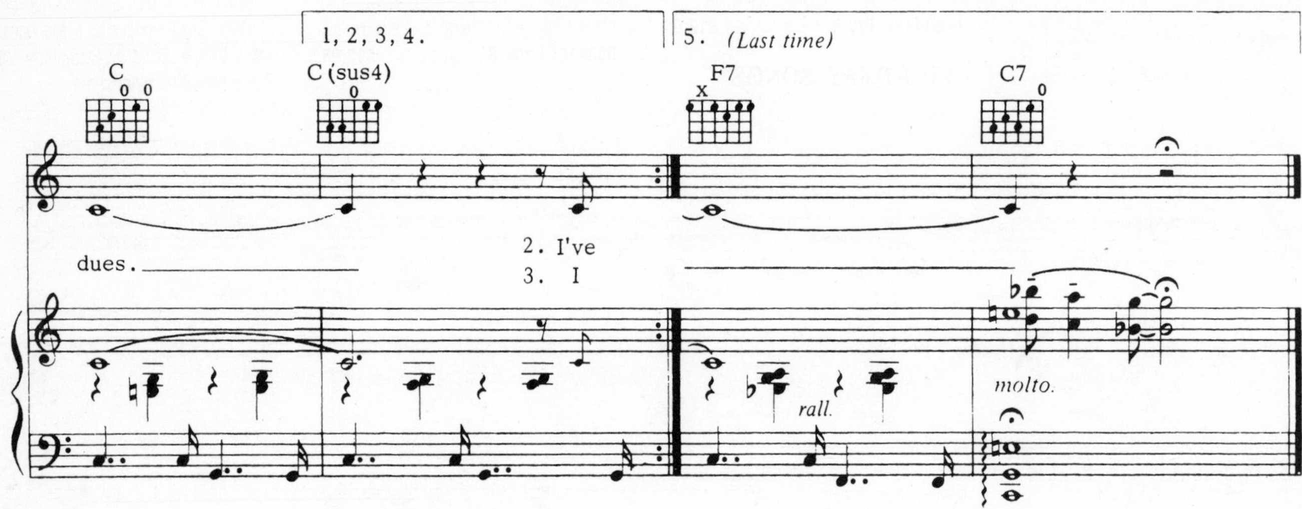

Extra verses:

4. *My kid's gonna grow up, gonna grow up to be a fool*
'Cause they ain't got no more room, no more room for him in school,
And everybody wants to know, why I sing the blues,
I say I've been around a long time, yes, I've really paid my dues.

5. *Yea, you know the company told me, yes, you're born to lose,*
Everybody around feel it, seems like everybody's got the blues.
But I had them a long time, I really, really paid my dues,
You know I ain't ashamed of it, people, I just love to sing the blues.